Better Homes and Gardens®

A Cross-Stitch CHRISTMAS™

Share the Joy

Better Homes and Gardens®
Des Moines, Iowa

A Cross-Stitch CHRISTMAS™

Editor-in-Chief *Beverly Rivers*
Managing Editor *Marjon Schaefer*
Art Director *Mary Bendgen*
Associate Art Director *Maureen Miller*

Assistant Art Director *Cherie DeTolve-Dale*
Associate Editor *Barbara Hickey*
Editorial Assistant *Jennifer Summers*

Contributing Graphic Design *Pattee Design*
Illustrator *Chris Neubauer Graphics*

V. P., Publishing Director *Max Runciman*
Publisher *William R. Reed*
Mktg./Ancillary Sales Director *Maureen Ruth*
Business Manager *Janet Donnelly*
Customer Service Manager *Karen Smith*

Meredith CORPORATION

Chairman *Jack D. Rehm*
President and CEO *William T. Kerr*

Chairman of the Executive Committee
E.T. Meredith III

Meredith Publishing Group
Publishing Group President *Christopher M. Little*
Meredith Custom Marketing *Bill Murphy*
Circulation *Hal Oringer*
Operations *Dean Pieters*

Member

HOBBY INDUSTRY
ASSOCIATION

Our "Mark of Excellence" seal
assures you that every project in
this publication has been
constructed and checked under
the direction of the crafts experts
at Better Homes and Gardens®
Cross Stitch & Needlework™
magazine.

For book editorial questions, write
Better Homes and Gardens®
Cross Stitch & Needlework™,
1912 Grand Ave.,
Des Moines, IA 50309-3379;
phone 515/284-3623; fax 515/284-3884.

ISSN: 1081-468X
ISBN: 0-696-20651-X (hardcover)
ISBN: 0-696-20652-8 (softcover)

At Christmastime

we celebrate what we hold most dearly in our hearts—our beliefs, our heritage, and our traditions. And even though our celebrations may differ, we all share common reasons to love the season.

In this spirit of love and peace, we invite you to enjoy this delightful collection of holiday cross stitch projects. Why not tuck a few handstitched gifts under your tree to begin a wonderful new family tradition?

Our Christmas wish for you is that you'll share many special traditions with your family, friends, and loved ones. By giving beautiful gifts that come from your hands and your heart, we believe you Share the Joy!

Merry Christmas Banner, page 9

Nativity, page 32

Country Christmas Sampler, page 51

A Cross-Stitch CHRISTMAS™

MAKING SPIRITS BRIGHT

Herald the arrival of Christmas with holiday stitchery for your home. Brimming with tradition, these cross-stitch designs are every bit as delightful to look at as they are to stitch.

GIFTS OF GOOD TASTE

Surprise your friends with two great gifts in one! Delicious homemade or purchased treats make lasting impressions when you present them in decorative wrappings like the ones shown in this chapter.

A STORY TO STITCH

The splendor and dignity of the Nativity are beautifully captured in this striking cross-stitch design, complete with eight dimensional figures.

COUNTRY COMFORTS

Come home to the country this Christmas and celebrate the season of love, joy, and peace with our collection of homespun projects that'll surely win your heart!

DECK THE BOUGHS

Even when your Christmas tree already glistens from top to bottom with pretty ornaments, there's always room for another. On these pages, irresistable patterns abound!

SANTA MAGIC

Any Christmas would be incomplete without St. Nicholas making his magical appearance. Our collection of six delightful Santas cross-stitches up in time for Christmas decorating and gift giving.

SYMBOLS OF THE SEASON

Start your holiday handcrafting with a collage of cross-stitched Christmas symbols. Surround yourself with familiar seasonal motifs for the merriest Christmas ever!

DRESSED IN HOLIDAY STYLE

This holiday season, dress in spectacular style with our festive collection of stitched wearables and accessories.

Pipecleaner Elves, page 69

St. Nick, page 81

Christmas Rose Blouse, page 107

5

Making
SPIRITS
BRIGHT

Merrily laud the season with a unique collection of four delightful cross-stitch designs that verbally as well as pictorially proclaim the universal wish on most everyone's lips, "Merry Christmas!" The framed piece shown here, and the stocking, banner, and afghan on the following pages all vie for the number-one spot in your home.

With a burst of gleeful noise on their shiny French horns, the two charming children on this sampler proclaim the Holy Days officially begun. Designer Rae Wroth from Wrangell, Arkansas, has creatively married color and pattern on linen fabric, producing a design that reflects her joy and enthusiasm for the season. The Merry Christmas banner captures the scene in a painterly swath along three sides of the composition. Shaded letters form the alphabet across the center of the stitchery—why not use them to initial your carefully stitched gifts! Pealing bells at the top of the design remind us of their actual counterparts calling us to rejoice the most celebrated birthday of all times.

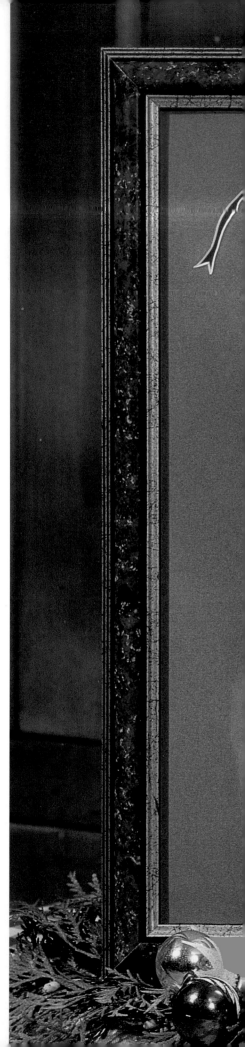

"The stockings were hung..." From the legend of St. Nicholas we learn that Nicholas, the benevolent bishop of Mira, Turkey, tossed some gold coins through an open window of the home of a poor father who had no dowry money for his three beautiful daughters. The coins landed in the young ladies' stockings which they had just washed and hung to dry. The stocking proceeded to become an important hiding place for small gifts, favors, and often, chocolate coins.

The Aida-cloth stocking, *opposite,* designed by Carole Rodgers, depicts what could be a scene viewed through a window of her Milo, Iowa, farmhouse—a bundled-up sleigh ride on an evergreen-lined country lane.

Create the beribboned welcoming banner, shown, *right,* even when precious stitching moments are hard to come by. Patricia Andrle from Collins, New York, used only one color of floss in her design so you can merrily stitch without having to decipher symbols or sort through your floss stash for that one elusive color! Sew a backing to the finished stitchery, then slip a padded board between the layers for a rigid, easy-to-hang holiday-home decoration.

MAKING SPIRITS BRIGHT

Designer Linda Gordanier-Jary, from Arlington, Texas, could not agree to one specific stitchery design, so she charted 10 different ones. She then stitched them onto the 11-count Aida squares of a large winter-white fringed afghan.

The bold folk art colors and shapes of these symbols of the season and their clearly spelled-out names ensure the afghan to become a popular one with tiny tikes who will be able to sound out the words and rattle off the colors to visiting holiday guests.

Worked separately, each design is particularly adaptable for use in a special handmade Christmas card. There are several card models available in the stitchery stores, and the handy thread-count exchange feature at the bottom of the color key will tell you which size fabric to buy.

MERRY CHRISTMAS SAMPLER

As shown on page 7.

Fabric and Thread

20×18" piece of 28-count white linen
Cotton embroidery floss in colors listed in key on *page 15*
Metallic thread in color listed in key on *page 15*

Supplies

Needle
Embroidery hoop
Desired frame and mat

Instructions

Zigzag-stitch or overcast the edges of the fabric to prevent fraying. Measure 4½" from the top and 4½" from the edge on the left side of the fabric; begin stitching the top left corner of the red border there with True Christmas red.

Use three plies of floss to work the cross-stitches over two threads of the fabric. Referring to the face-detail charts on *page 15,* work the petite half cross-stitches (over one thread) using one ply of floss. Work the straight stitches using one ply of floss unless otherwise specified in the key on *page 15.*

Use one strand of metallic gold thread to work the running stitches. Work the Smyrna cross stitches using one strand of metallic gold thread and referring to the diagram, *page 15.* Work the French knots in between the Smyrna cross-stitches using one ply of floss. Work the couching stitches as specified in the key on *page 15,* and referring to the diagram, *page 15.* Use one ply of floss to work the backstitches unless otherwise specified in the key. Press the finished stitchery from the back. Mat and frame the piece as desired.

SLEIGH STOCKING

As shown on page 8, the finished stocking is 18"-long.

Fabric and Thread

26×20" piece of 14 count white Aida cloth
1¾ yards of 45"-wide Christmas-print fabric
20×18" piece of fusible fleece
8×16" piece of fusible fleece
Cotton embroidery floss in colors listed in the key on *page 16*
#8 braid in color listed in key on *page 16*

Supplies

Graph paper
Pencil
Needle
Embroidery hoop
Air-soluble fabric marker
48" length of ¼"-wide pink twisted cord
64" length of ⅝"-wide metallic gold-and-black flat lace
Twenty-four ½"-diameter gold jingle bells

Instructions

Chart the desired initials using the alphabet on *page 18,* and separating each letter by three squares. Zigzag-stitch or overcast the edges of the Aida cloth to prevent fraying. Measure 8" from the top of the fabric. Find the vertical center of the chart and the fabric, begin stitching the top of the frame motif there.

Center and stitch the desired initials inside the frame motif. Use three plies of floss or one strand of the braid to work the cross-stitches. Work the French knots as specified in the key. Work the backstitches using one ply of floss.

Use the air-soluble marker to draw the stocking outline around the stitched area. Fuse the large piece of fleece to the back of the Aida cloth stocking area. Cut out the stocking ½" beyond the marked lines.

Use the stocking as a pattern to cut one matching back and two lining pieces from the Christmas-print fabric. Also cut one 2×6" hanging strip, one 8×16" cuff, and one 7×45" bow from the Christmas-print fabric.

All measurements include a ½" seam allowance.

With edges even, baste the lace along the sides and foot of the stitched stocking front. Sew the stitched stocking front to the fabric back, right sides together, along the basting lines, leaving the top edge open. Turn the stocking right side out. Hand-stitch the pink cord to the front of the stocking, between the stitched front and the lace.

Fuse the remaining piece of fleece to the back of the cuff piece. With right sides together and raw edges even, sew the short ends of the cuff piece together. Fold the cuff in half right side out; press. Baste the raw edges of the cuff to the top of the stocking.

Press under ¼" at the long edges of the hanging strip. Fold the hanging strip in half lengthwise; top-stitch. Fold the strip in half to form a loop; tack the loop inside the top left side of the stocking.

Sew the lining pieces together, leaving the top open and leaving a 3" opening at the bottom of the foot; do not turn. With right sides together, slip the stocking inside the lining. Stitch the stocking to the lining at the top edges.

Carefully pull the stocking out through the opening in the toe. Slip-stitch the opening closed. Tuck the lining into the stocking and fold the cuff down; press.

For the bow, fold the 7×45" strip in half lengthwise, right sides together. Taper and cut the ends to a point; stitch, leaving an opening in the center. Turn right side out; press. Tie the fabric into a bow; tack to the top left side of the stocking. Baste the remaining lace along the edge of the cuff. Sew 21 jingle bells at evenly-spaced intervals around the cuff, ½" from the edge. Sew three jingle bells to the center of the bow.

VERY MERRY CHRISTMAS BANNER

As shown on page 9.

Fabric and Thread
18×22" piece of 20-count gold-and-cream Valerie fabric
1¼ yards of 45"-wide red satin fabric
13⅜×17" piece of fleece
Variegated cotton embroidery floss in color listed in key on *page 18*
Kreinik blending filament in color listed in the key on *page 18*

Supplies
Needle
Embroidery hoop
Matching sewing threads
2 yards of ⅝"-wide red satin ribbon
Fifteen ⅝"-diameter gold jingle bells
Two purchased 3"-long gold tassels
1¾ yards of ½"-diameter piping cord
1¾ yards of ¼"-diameter metallic gold twisted cord
11¾×15¼" piece of foam mounting board
Purchased 16"-long wood decorator dowel
Purchased 27"-long ¼"-diameter gold drapery cord with tassels
Crafts glue

Instructions
Zigzag-stitch or overcast the edges of the fabric to prevent fraying. Measure 4½" from the top and 7" from the edge on the left side of the fabric; begin working the top stitch of the "A" there. Blend three plies of floss and one strand of filament to work the cross-stitches over two threads of the fabric. Work a basting-stitch rectangle around the design 2½" beyond the stitched area. Trim the Valerie fabric ½" beyond the basting stitches. Use the Valerie as a pattern to cut a matching back from the red satin fabric. From the red satin fabric also cut a 2×13¾" dowel sleeve and a 2¾×60" bias piping strip, piecing strips as necessary.

All measurements include a ½" seam allowance. All seams are sewn together with the right sides facing unless it is otherwise specified.

Baste the fleece to the wrong side of the stitchery. To make piping, fold the red bias strip over the piping cord. Use a zipper foot to sew through both fabric layers next to the piping cord.

Pin the piping along the edges of the stitchery, with right sides together and raw edges even. Sew close to the piping, using a zipper foot. (Leave 1" of the piping free where the ends meet; cut the piping cord so the ends meet. Trim the fabric, leaving enough to turn under ½"; hand-sew the fabric ends together. Finish stitching the piping to the edge.)

For the dowel sleeve, fold under 1" at both short ends of the strip; press. Fold the strip in half lengthwise with wrong sides together. Centered and with the top raw edges even, pin the dowel sleeve to the top front, over the piping; stitch. Hand-sew the gold cord between the stitchery and the piping, with ends meeting at the center bottom. Wrap thread around the ends of the cord several times before cutting and put glue on the ends to prevent fraying.

Press under ½" at the top edge of the satin back piece; baste. Sew the front to the back with right sides together and raw edges even and leaving the entire top edge open. Trim the fleece and corners. Turn right side out and press. Insert the foam mounting board into the top opening. Turn under and whipstitch the back to the stitching line of the sleeve to close.

Fold the red satin ribbon in half. Referring to the photograph on *page 9*, tack the folded edge of the ribbon centered vertically between the "A" and the "e" and 23 threads above the "e" in "Merry". Working on the right side of the design, fold the ribbon at the second marking. Tack the ribbon in place with a gold jingle bell. Continue to tack the ribbon at the markings, folding the ribbon at each new position before securing with a gold jingle bell. Repeat for the opposite side of the design.

Sew the two gold tassels to the bottom of the design where the ribbon ends meet. Sew three jingle bells above the tassels. Trim the ribbon ends. Insert the dowel through the sleeve. Tie the ends of the drapery cord around each end of the dowel.

STITCHING ON AFGHANS

Cross-stitching on afghan fabric may be quite a challenge, even for a seasoned stitcher. We've asked Pat Carson from Designs by Gloria & Pat, Inc. to give us some tips on how to obtain the best results.

1. Be sure to stitch on the side of the fabric with the raised pattern.
2. Each square on a cross-stitch chart equals two threads of an afghan fabric. To ensure even stitches when working on even-weave fabric, begin stitching next to a vertical thread, bringing the needle up where a vertical thread crosses a horizontal thread and taking the needle down two threads up and over, again where a vertical thread crosses a horizontal thread.
3. Buy enough of each floss color at one time to ensure the same dye lot will be used throughout the project.
4. Separate the six-strand embroidery floss into individual strands, then combine as many stands as the instructions specify. This will help the floss lie more smoothly on your afghan.
5. Do not turn your fabric 90 degrees, because your stitches will not cross in the same direction. You may turn the fabric and the chart 180 degrees.
6. End threads by weaving them vertically through stitches on the back of the afghan fabric.
7. Stitch the center motif first, then the border.
8. Fringe the afghan when stitching is complete.
9. Afghan fabrics are not meant to be lined or backed with a fusible facing.

Merry Christmas Sampler

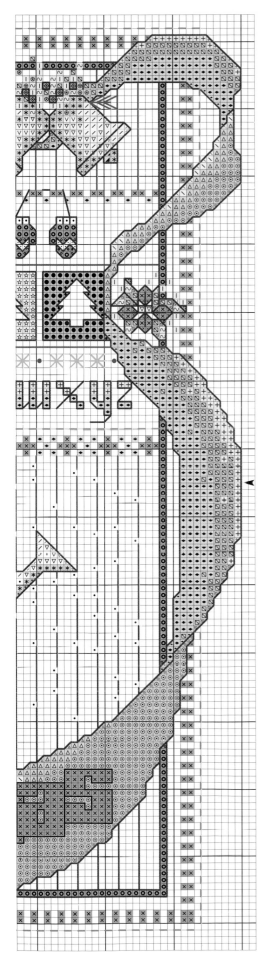

MERRY CHRISTMAS SAMPLER

Anchor		DMC	
002	·	000	White
1006	◈	304	Medium Christmas red
9046	✕	321	True Christmas red
214	+	368	Light pistachio
358	◢	433	Dark chestnut
877	⊙	502	Medium blue green
875	△	503	True blue green
1042	⟍	504	Pale blue green
280	⊛	581	Moss green
8581	◆	646	Medium beaver gray
886	⁄	677	Pale old gold
901	✳	680	Dark old gold
305	☆	725	Topaz
890	▽	729	Medium old gold
132	●	797	Light royal blue
136	◇	799	Medium Delft blue
043	▼	814	Dark garnet
1005	◐	816	Light garnet
380	#	838	Deep beige brown
360	⊖	839	Dark beige brown
379	▢	840	Medium beige brown
862	◆	934	Deep pine green
847	▽	3072	Pale beaver gray
267	◨	3346	Light hunter green
266	∿	3347	Medium yellow green
264	Ɪ	3348	Light yellow green
382	▲	3371	Black brown

PETITE HALF CROSS-STITCH

1022	▢	760	True salmon
1021	⦂	761	Light salmon
131	⊕	798	Dark Delft blue
1020	⊟	3713	Pale salmon

BACKSTITCH

403	⁄	310	Black
9046	⁄	321	True Christmas red
043	⁄	814	Dark garnet
1005	⁄	816	Light garnet
382	⁄	3371	Black brown—Merry Christmas lettering (2X); alphabet and numerals (1X)

STRAIGHT STITCH

268	⁄	3345	Dark yellow green

FRENCH KNOT

9046	●	321	True Christmas red

SMYRNA STITCH

	✳	284	Metallic gold

RUNNING STITCH

	– –	284	Metallic gold

COUCHING STITCH

382	⁄	3371	Black brown—handle
		284	Metallic gold – scarf fringe

Stitch count: 132 high x 119 wide
Finished design sizes:
28-count fabric – 9½ x 8½ inches
22-count fabric – 12 x 10⅞ inches
36-count fabric – 7⅓ x 6⅝ inches

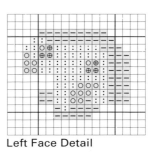

Left Face Detail

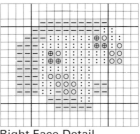

Right Face Detail

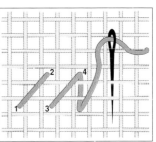

Half Cross-Stitch

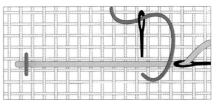

Couching Stitch

Smyrna Cross Stitch

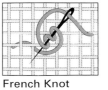

French Knot

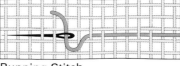

Running Stitch

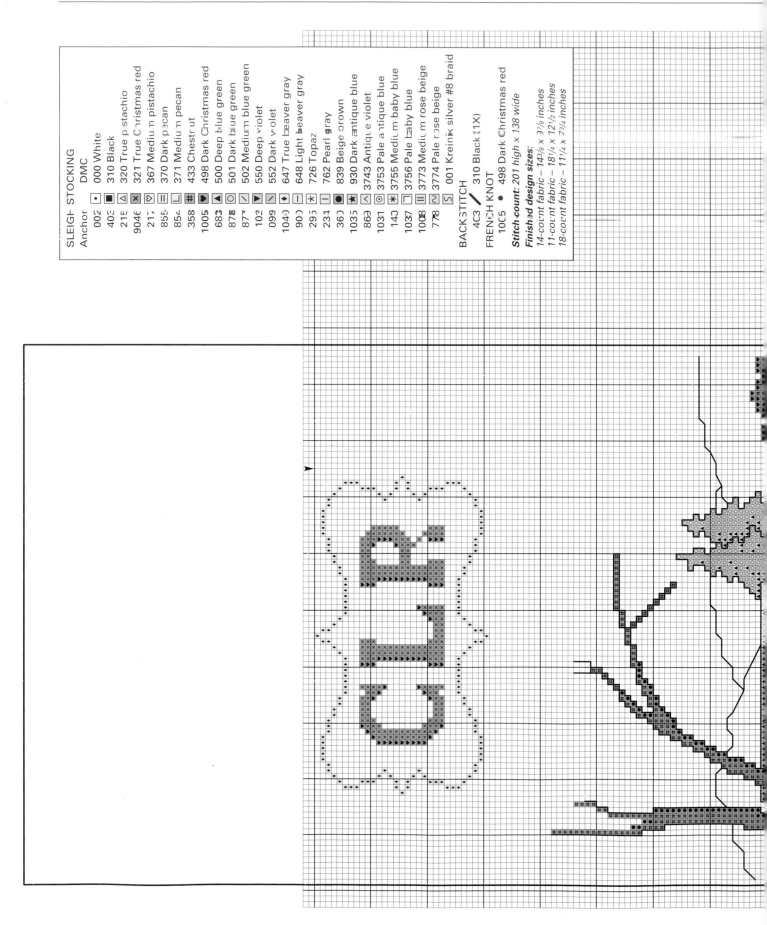

SLEIGH STOCKING

Anchor		DMC	
002	·	000	White
403	■	310	Black
215	△	320	True pistachio
9046	✕	321	True Christmas red
217	▷	367	Medium pistachio
855	=	370	Dark pecan
854	⌐	371	Medium pecan
358	#	433	Chestnut
1005	▶	498	Dark Christmas red
683	◀	500	Deep blue green
878	○	501	Dark blue green
877	/	502	Medium blue green
102	▶	550	Deep violet
099	/	552	Dark violet
1040	◆	647	True beaver gray
900			648	Light beaver gray
295	✱	726	Topaz
234	—	762	Pearl gray
360	●	839	Beige brown
1035	★	930	Dark antique blue
862	◁	3743	Antique violet
1031	⊙	3753	Pale antique blue
140	✱	3755	Medium baby blue
1037	⌐	3756	Pale baby blue
1008	=	3773	Medium rose beige
778	⌐	3774	Pale rose beige
	S	001	Kreinik silver #8 braid

BACKSTITCH
4C3 / 310 Black (1X)
10C5 ● 498 Dark Christmas red

FRENCH KNOT

Stitch count: 201 high x 138 wide
Finished design sizes:
14-count fabric – 14⅜ x ⅞ inches
11-count fabric – 18¼ x 12½ inches
18-count fabric – 11¼ x 7¾ inches

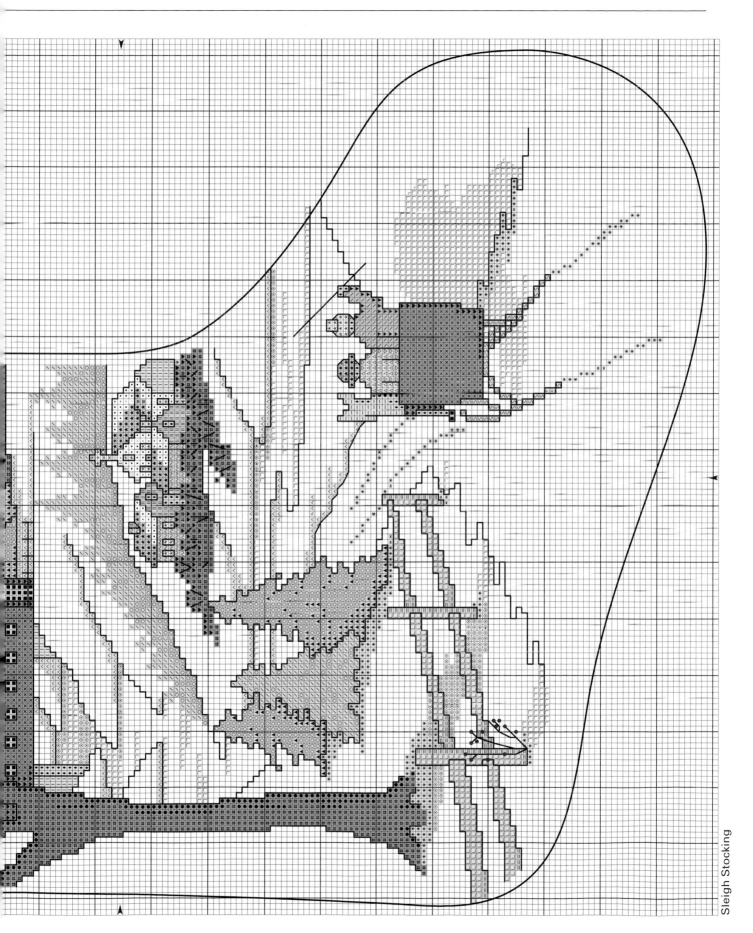

Sleigh Stocking

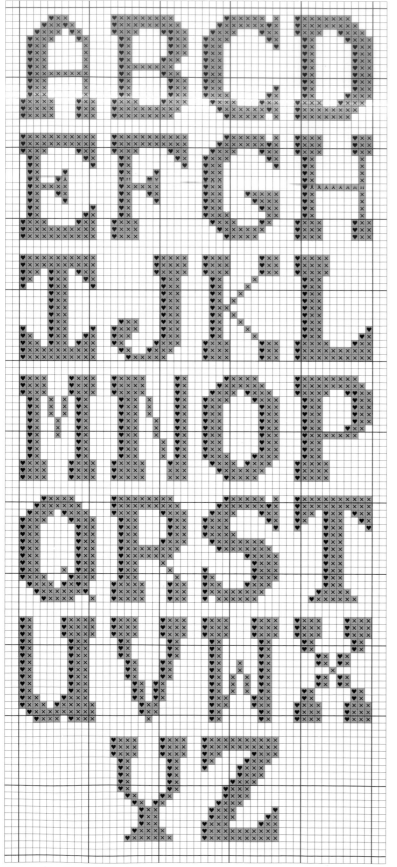

Sleigh Stocking Alphabet

SLEIGH STOCKING

Anchor		DMC	
002	·	000	White
403	■	310	Black
215	△	320	True pistachio
9046	✕	321	True Christmas red
217	♡	367	Medium pistachio
855	=	370	Dark pecan
854	∟	371	Medium pecan
358	#	433	Chestnut
1005	♥	498	Dark Christmas red
683	▲	500	Deep blue green
878	○	501	Dark blue green
877	╱	502	Medium blue green
102	▼	550	Deep violet
099	╲	552	Dark violet
1040	◆	647	True beaver gray
900	—	648	Light beaver gray
295	★	726	Topaz
234	I	762	Pearl gray
360	●	839	Beige brown
1035	★	930	Dark antique blue
869	∧	3743	Antique violet
1031	⊙	3753	Pale antique blue
140	✱	3755	Medium baby blue
1037	⌐	3756	Pale baby blue
1008	II	3773	Medium rose beige
778	∼	3774	Pale rose beige
	S	001	Kreinik silver #8 braid

BACKSTITCH

403	╱	310 Black (1X)

FRENCH KNOT

1005	●	498 Dark Christmas red

Stitch count: 201 high x 138 wide

Finished design sizes:
14-count fabric – 14³/₈ x 9⁷/₈ inches
11-count fabric – 18¹/₄ x 12¹/₂ inches
18-count fabric – 11¹/₄ x 7³/₄ inches

**HOLIDAY WELCOME
BANNER**

Anchor		DMC	
1206	✕	115	Variegated red (3X) and 003 Kreinik red blending filament (1X)

JINGLE BELLS

—	10mm brass bells

Stitch count: 118 high x 85 wide
Finished design sizes:
20-count fabric – 11⁷/₈ x 8¹/₂ inches
28-count fabric – 8¹/₂ x 6¹/₈ inches
32-count fabric – 7³/₈ x 5³/₈ inches

A Very Merry Christmas to All!

Holiday Welcome Banner

COUNTRY CHRISTMAS AFGHAN

As shown on page 11.

Fabric and Floss

Purchased 50×60" 14-count antique white Lady Elizabeth afghan

Cotton embroidery floss in colors listed in key

One additional skein *each* of medium old gold (DMC 729) and deep watermelon (DMC 3801), two additional skeins of white (DMC 000), three additional skeins of true Christmas red (DMC 321), and five additional skeins of true emerald (DMC 910)

Kreinik #8 braid in color listed in key

Supplies

Tapestry needle

3⅓ yards of ⅞"-wide red satin ribbon

Instructions

Refer to the photograph, *pages 10-11*, to position the motifs. Locate the center of one square on the afghan and the center of the first motif chart; begin stitching there. Use six plies of floss or two strands of braid to work the cross-stitches over two threads of the afghan. Work the backstitches using two plies of floss.

For the fringe, topstitch around all four sides, 3½" from the edges of the afghan. Remove the threads to the topstitching. Cut ten 12" pieces from the red satin ribbon. Tie each ribbon into a bow. Tack a bow to the center of each unstitched square of the afghan. (***Note:** Additional skeins of floss will be needed for the main colors of any motif that is stitched more than one time.*)

COUNTRY CHRISTMAS AFGHAN

Anchor		DMC
002	•	000 White
215	S	320 True pistachio
9046	♥	321 Christmas red
214	/	368 Light pistachio
235	●	414 Steel
398	∧	415 Light pearl gray
891	◇	676 Light old gold
238	‖	703 Chartreuse
323	◈	722 Light bittersweet
890	◉	729 Medium old gold
302	○	743 True yellow
301	⊡	744 Medium yellow
300	⊡	745 Light yellow
275	⊟	746 Off-white
1021	⊓	761 Light salmon
234	◺	762 Pale pearl gray
307	⊞	783 Christmas gold
1005	★	816 Light garnet
360	✳	839 Dark beige brown
379	△	840 Medium beige brown
052	✶	899 Rose
229	✕	910 True emerald
209	L	912 Light emerald
1011	⊟	948 Peach
1020	☆	3713 Pale salmon
035	◎	3801 Watermelon
923	▲	3818 Deep emerald
306	♥	3820 Dark straw
305	▽	3821 True straw
	▢	002 Kreinik gold #8 braid

BACKSTITCH

218	/	319 Dark pistachio – mittens, angel dress, candle greenery, wreath, spruce
217	/	367 Medium pistachio – mistletoe leaves
235	/	414 Steel – snowman, candle, hearts button
891	/	676 Light old gold – mistletoe berries
324	/	721 Medium bittersweet – snowman nose
310	/	780 Deep topaz – spruce sled
308	/	782 Medium topaz – hearts star, candle flame, horn
307	/	783 Christmas gold – angel hair
045	/	814 Dark garnet – ribbons, heart, candle berries, sled
1005	/	816 Light garnet – snowman heart and mouth, angel heart and mouth
380	/	838 Deep beige brown – snowman hat, buttons, eyes, candle holder, tree trunk
360	/	839 Dark beige brown – bird house, angel eyes and nose, wreath buttons
379	/	840 Medium beige brown – angel chin and hands
306	/	3820 Dark straw – angel wings

STRAIGHT STITCH

380	/	838 Deep beige brown – candle berries
379	/	840 Medium beige brown – mistletoe berries

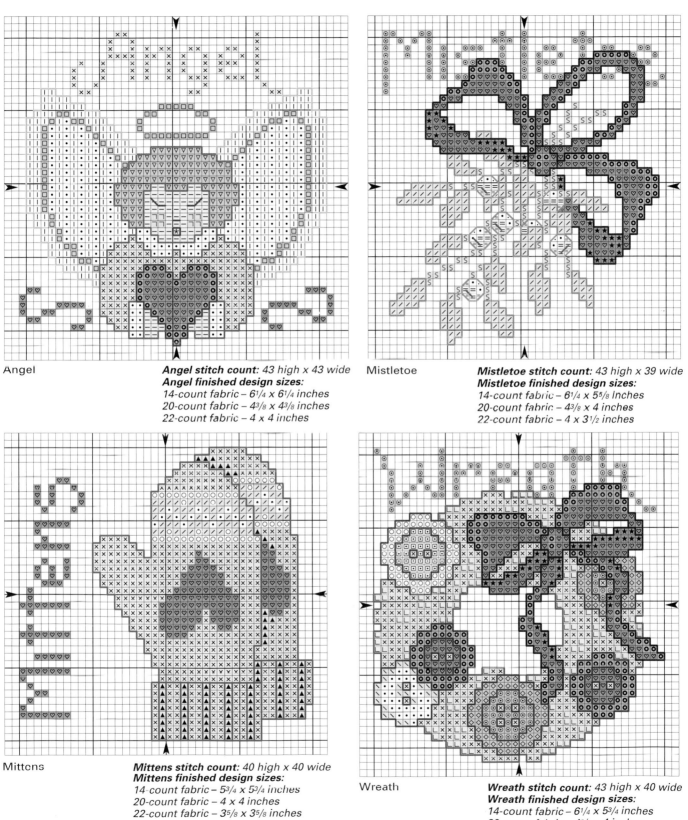

Angel

Angel stitch count: *43 high x 43 wide*
Angel finished design sizes:
14-count fabric – 6¼ x 6¼ inches
20-count fabric – 4⅜ x 4⅜ inches
22-count fabric – 4 x 4 inches

Mistletoe

Mistletoe stitch count: *43 high x 39 wide*
Mistletoe finished design sizes:
14-count fabric – 6¼ x 5⅝ inches
20-count fabric – 4⅜ x 4 inches
22-count fabric – 4 x 3½ inches

Mittens

Mittens stitch count: *40 high x 40 wide*
Mittens finished design sizes:
14-count fabric – 5¾ x 5¾ inches
20-count fabric – 4 x 4 inches
22-count fabric – 3⅝ x 3⅝ inches

Wreath

Wreath stitch count: *43 high x 40 wide*
Wreath finished design sizes:
14-count fabric – 6¼ x 5¾ inches
20-count fabric – 4⅜ x 4 inches
22-count fabric – 4 x 3⅝ inches

COUNTRY CHRISTMAS AFGHAN

Anchor		DMC	
002	⊡	000	White
215	S	320	True pistachio
9046	♡	321	Christmas red
214	⟋	368	Light pistachio
235	●	414	Steel
398	∧	415	Light pearl gray
891	◇	676	Light old gold
238	‖	703	Chartreuse
323	∼	722	Light bittersweet
890	◉	729	Medium old gold
302	○	743	True yellow
301	⊡	744	Medium yellow
300	⊔	745	Light yellow
275	⊟	746	Off-white
1021	⌐	761	Light salmon
234	＼	762	Pale pearl gray
307	＃	783	Christmas gold
1005	★	816	Light garnet
360	✳	839	Dark beige brown
379	△	840	Medium beige brown
052	✴	899	Rose
229	✕	910	True emerald
209	∟	912	Light emerald
1011	⊟	948	Peach
1020	✪	3713	Pale salmon
035	◑	3801	Watermelon
923	▲	3818	Deep emerald
306	♥	3820	Dark straw
305	▽	3821	True straw
	☐	002	Kreinik gold #8 braid

BACKSTITCH

218	⟋	319 Dark pistachio – mittens, angel dress, candle greenery, wreath, spruce
217	⟋	367 Medium pistachio – mistletoe leaves
235	⟋	414 Steel – snowman, candle, hearts button
891	⟋	676 Light old gold – mistletoe berries
324	⟋	721 Medium bittersweet – snowman nose
310	⟋	780 Deep topaz – spruce sled
308	⟋	782 Medium topaz – hearts star, candle flame, horn
307	⟋	783 Christmas gold – angel hair
045	⟋	814 Dark garnet – ribbons, heart, candle berries, sled
1005	⟋	816 Light garnet – snowman heart and mouth, angel heart and mouth
380	⟋	838 Deep beige brown – snowman hat, buttons, eyes, candle holder, tree trunk
360	⟋	839 Dark beige brown – bird house, angel eyes and nose, wreath buttons
379	⟋	840 Medium beige brown – angel chin and hands
306	⟋	3820 Dark straw – angel wings

STRAIGHT STITCH

380	⟋	838 Deep beige brown – candle berries
379	⟋	840 Medium beige brown – mistletoe berries

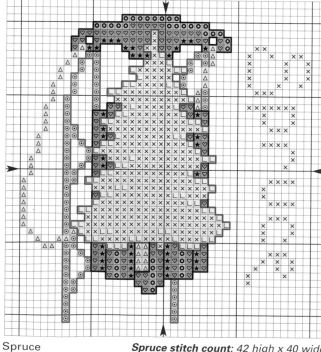

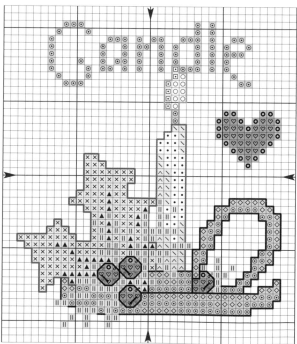

Spruce

Spruce stitch count: *42 high x 40 wide*
Spruce finished design sizes:
14-count fabric – 6 x 5³⁄₄ inches
20-count fabric – 4¹⁄₄ x 4 inches
22-count fabric – 3⁷⁄₈ x 3⁵⁄₈ inches

Candle

Candle stitch count: *42 high x 36 wide*
Candle finished design sizes:
14-count fabric – 6 x 5¹⁄₄ inches
20-count fabric – 4¹⁄₄ x 3⁵⁄₈ inches
22-count fabric – 3⁷⁄₈ x 3¹⁄₄ inches

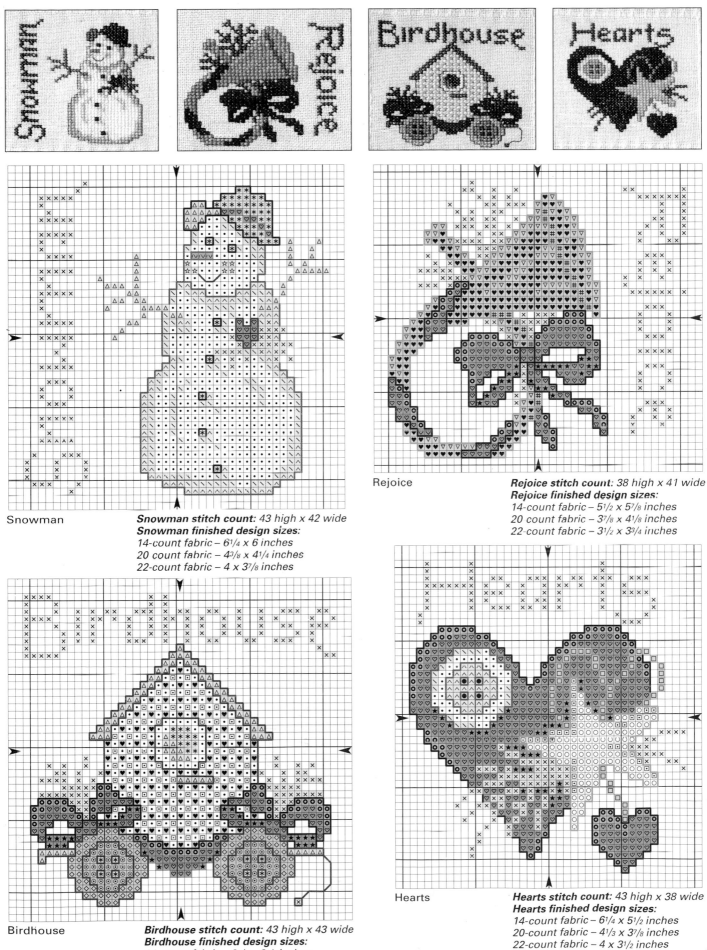

Snowman

Snowman stitch count: *43 high x 42 wide*
Snowman finished design sizes:
14-count fabric – 6¼ x 6 inches
20 count fabric – 4⅜ x 4¼ inches
22-count fabric – 4 x 3⅞ inches

Rejoice

Rejoice stitch count: *38 high x 41 wide*
Rejoice finished design sizes:
14-count fabric – 5½ x 5⅞ inches
20 count fabric – 3⅞ x 4⅛ inches
22-count fabric – 3½ x 3¾ inches

Birdhouse

Birdhouse stitch count: *43 high x 43 wide*
Birdhouse finished design sizes:
14-count fabric – 6¼ x 6¼ inches
20 count fabric – 4⅜ x 4⅜ inches
22-count fabric – 4 x 4 inches

Hearts

Hearts stitch count: *43 high x 38 wide*
Hearts finished design sizes:
14-count fabric – 6¼ x 5½ inches
20 count fabric – 4⅓ x 3⅞ inches
22-count fabric – 4 x 3½ inches

23

Gifts of
GOOD TASTE

Turn tasty tokens of appreciation into meaningful gifts

from your hand when you package or serve the treats

in containers accented with cross-stitch. On these

and the following pages, designers share their talents

with you in the form of three different and mostly

red-and-white banding motifs, a Christmas-rose bouquet

of table enhancers, and a trio of tiny gift sacks.

Three designs to inspire a wealth of application ideas. That's what our designers had in mind when they charted these bright and bouncy motifs to decorate last-minute gifts. Designer Beth McNeece from Lolo, Montana, stitched hers on Aida banding—how about stitching the popcorn-and-cranberry garland on a frayed strip of jute to weave in and out the branches of a welcoming wreath? And can you see the spirited Santas by Barbara Sestok of Germantown, New York, tumbling down the center front of your favorite denim shirt, laughing all the way? Stitch a plastic canvas sheet full of peppermint candies, by Woodstock, Georgia's Helen Nicholson, then cut out the candies and wrap them in cellophane for tree decorations, or glue onto barrettes, button covers, and tiny magnets. All would make wonderful tokens of spirited gift-giving.

gift from the heart is often handmade. Why not let loved ones know how much they mean to you by surprising them with an ensemble of table accents that's sure to serve up a special helping of Christmas cheer. Laura Doyle from Floral Park, New York, combined bright

red berries with pink roses on quick-to-stitch ivory Royal Classic fabric—a holiday bouquet to delight stitcher and recipient alike.

teddy in a wreath and a rosy-cheek snowman keep Jolly Santa company on this trio of 28-count Jobelan-fabric

bags. Project designer Laura Doyle supplies three Christmas-ready motifs to stitch on any fabric you prefer—choose a 22-count fabric for a sack large enough to hold a stash of chocolate-chip cookies. With three designs to choose from, the most difficult part will be deciding which one to stitch first!

CHRISTMAS GIFT BAGS

As shown on page 27.

Fabric and Floss
for each bag
8×18" piece of 28-count white
    Jobelan fabric
Cotton embroidery floss in colors
    listed in the key, *far right*
5½×15" piece of Christmas print
    fabric
5½×15" piece of lightweight
    fusible interfacing

Supplies
Needle: embroidery hoop

Instructions
Zigzag-stitch or overcast the edges of the Jobelan fabric to prevent fraying. Locate the vertical center of the desired chart and the vertical center of one piece of fabric. Measure down 2" from the top of the fabric's vertical center; begin stitching the top row of the chart there. Use three plies of floss to work the cross-stitches over two threads of the fabric. Work the Algerian eyelets on the Santa with two plies of floss, elongating some of the "legs" as shown on the chart. Work the straight stitches as specified in the key. Work the backstitches using one ply of floss. Press the finished stitchery from the back.

Centering the design and leaving a ¾" margin on the sides and 1½" at the top of the design, trim the fabric to measure 5½×15". Fuse the interfacing to the wrong side of the stitchery, following manufacturer's instructions. Fold the fabric in half with right sides together. Sew the side edges of the fabric together with a ¼" seam allowance; *do not* turn.

To shape the bottom corners, match the side seams and fold a corner, making a point on one side of the bag. (See the diagram, *page 31.*)

Measure ½" from the point and make a mark across the point. Machine-stitch across the point on the marked line; trim. Repeat to make the other corner of the bag bottom; set aside.

Sew a Christmas-print lining by following the same instructions as for the Jobelan fabric bag. Stitch the lining to the bag at the top edges with right sides together and turn. Slip-stitch the opening closed. Tuck the lining into bag; press carefully.

ROSE BREADCLOTH, NAPKIN, AND JAR TOPPER

As shown on page 26.

Fabric and Floss
18×18" 14-count ivory Royal
    Classic breadcloth
15×15" 14-count ivory Royal
    Classic napkin
For Jar Topper
6×6" piece of 14-count ivory Aida
    cloth
⅙ yard of 45"-wide rose print
    fabric
6"-diameter circle of lightweight
    fusible interfacing
Cotton embroidery floss in colors
    listed in the key on *page 30*

Supplies
Needle
For Jar Topper
Matching sewing thread
24"-length of ¹⁄₁₆"-diameter
    elastic cord
20"-length of ¼"-wide rose
    satin ribbon

Instructions
Measure 1½" from the left edge and ½" from the bottom of the breadcloth; begin stitching the bottom row of the leaf on the large rose chart there. For the napkin, meaure 1" from the bottom and 1½" from left edge; begin working the left stitch of the bottom row there. Use three plies of floss to work the cross-stitches. Work the backstitches using one ply of floss.

For the jar topper, zigzag-stitch or overcast the edges of the Aida cloth to prevent fraying. Find the center of the chart and the Aida cloth; begin stitching there. Use three plies of floss to work the cross-stitches. Work the backstitches using one ply of floss. Center and fuse the interfacing to the back of the Aida cloth following the manufacturer's instructions. Centering the design, baste a 4"-diameter circle on the Aida cloth.

Cut a 3⅛×37" strip from the rose print fabric. With right sides together, sew the short ends of the strip, forming a continuous loop. Sew a ⅛" hem in one long edge of the strip. Run gathering threads ⅜" and ¼" from the other long edge of the strip. On the wrong side of the fabric, secure one end of the elastic cord 1" from the hemmed edge, then, machine-zigzag stitch over the elastic cord, pulling the cord as you stitch. Tighten the elastic to fit the jar. Secure the free end of the elastic by sewing across the cord.

Gather the ruffle to fit the perimeter of the Aida circle. With right sides together, baste the ruffle to the Aida cloth. Trim the Aida cloth even with the ruffle's edge. Adjust the gathers and stitch. Slip the topper over the jar. Tie the ribbon around the topper.

POPCORN GARLAND, HO HO SANTA, AND PEPPERMINT CANDY BANDING

As shown on pages 24 and 25.

Fabric and Floss
2½"-wide 16-count Aida banding
    with bow border in color of
    your choice
Cotton embroidery floss in colors
    listed in the keys *opposite*
Kreinik blending filament in colors
    listed in the key *opposite*

Supplies
Needle

Instructions
Locate the horizontal center of the desired chart and the banding. Measure 1" from one end of the banding; begin stitching there. Use three plies of floss to work the cross-stitches. Work the backstitches using one ply of floss. For the Peppermint Candy design, work the blended needle stitches as specified in the key on *page 31*. Repeat the motifs until the desired length is reached. Press the finished stitchery from the back.

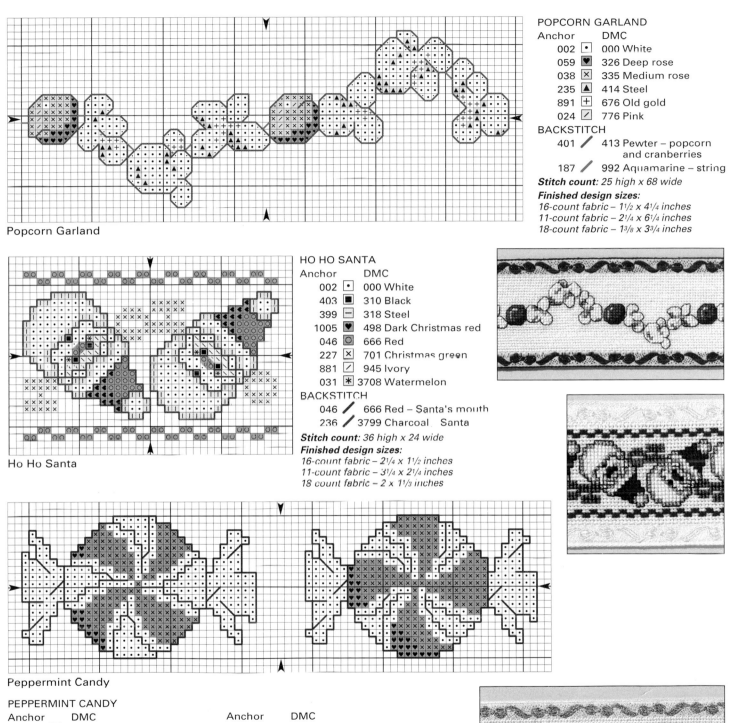

Popcorn Garland

Ho Ho Santa

Peppermint Candy

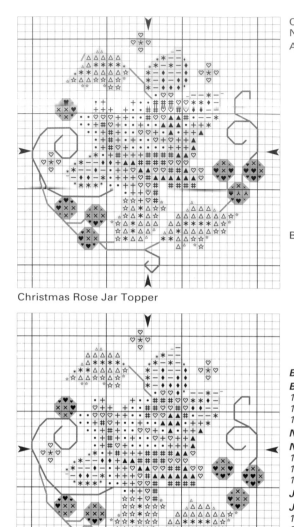

Christmas Rose Jar Topper

Christmas Rose Napkin

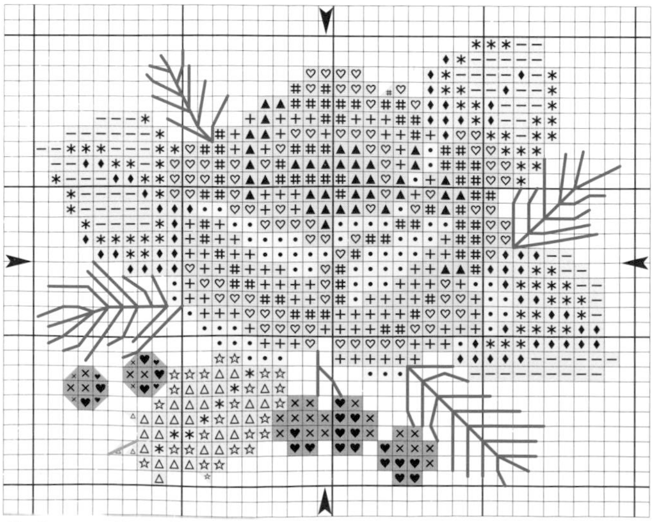

Christmas Rose Breadcloth

CHRISTMAS ROSE BREAD CLOTH, NAPKIN, AND JAR TOPPER

Anchor		DMC	
9046	☒	321	Christmas red
267	☆	470	Medium avocado
266	△	471	Light avocado
307	✳	783	Christmas gold
043	♥	815	Garnet
218	◆	890	Pistachio
075	♡	962	Medium rose pink
073	•	963	Pale rose pink
244	✱	987	Medium forest green
242	−	989	Pale forest green
059	▲	3350	Deep dusty rose
025	+	3716	Light rose pink
076	#	3731	Dark dusty rose

BACKSTITCH

267	/	470	Medium avocado – stems, vines
266	/	471	Light avocado – leaf on bread cloth, jar topper
923	/	699	Christmas green – pine branches (2X)
244	/	987	Medium forest green – vine
242	/	989	Pale forest green – leaf

Bread cloth stitch count: 30 high x 39 wide
Bread cloth finished design sizes:
14-count fabric – 2¼ x 2¾ inches
11-count fabric – 2¾ x 3½ inches
18-count fabric – 1⅔ x 2¼ inches
Napkin stitch count: 32 high x 31 wide
Napkin finished design sizes:
14-count fabric – 2¼ x 2¼ inches
11-count fabric – 3 x 2⅞ inches
18-count fabric – 1¾ x 1¾ inches
Jar Topper stitch count: 32 high x 31 wide
Jar Topper finished design sizes:
14-count fabric – 2¼ x 2¼ inches
11-count fabric – 3 x 2⅞ inches
18-count fabric – 1¾ x 1¾ inches

BEAR, SNOWMAN, AND SANTA GIFT BAGS

Anchor		DMC	
002	•	000	White
403	■	310	Black
9046	+	321	Christmas red
009	S	352	Coral
008	□	353	Dark peach
398	✳	415	Light pearl gray
267	⊙	470	Medium avocado
266	−	471	Light avocado
1012	✓	754	Medium peach
234	◣	762	Pale pearl gray
128	▽	775	Baby blue
307	U	783	Christmas gold
176	▲	793	Cornflower blue
043	♥	815	Garnet
162	●	825	Bright blue
378	◇	841	True beige brown
388	I	842	Light beige brown
246	#	986	Dark forest green
242	◢	989	Pale forest green
036	☒	3326	Rose

BACKSTITCH

403	/	310	Black – snowman hat, all eyes, bear mouth and nose
9046	/	321	Christmas red – wreath flowers, snowman nose and mouth, scarf fringe
398	/	415	Light pearl gray – Santa
043	/	815	Garnet – snowman jacket
162	/	825	Bright blue – snowman, scarf, snow
378	/	841	True beige brown – bear
246	/	986	Dark forest green – tree

STRAIGHT STITCH

307	/	783	Christmas gold – star on tree
246	/	986	Dark forest green – tree

ALGERIAN EYELET

176	✳	793	Cornflower blue – Santa gift bag (2X)

Bear stitch count: 64 high x 55 wide
Bear finished design sizes:
28-count fabric – 4½ x 4 inches
22-count fabric – 5⅞ x 5 inches
36-count fabric – 3½ x 3 inches
Santa stitch count: 64 high x 55 wide
Santa finished design sizes:
28-count fabric – 4½ x 4 inches
22-count fabric – 5⅞ x 5 inches
36-count fabric – 3½ x 3 inches
Snowman stitch count: 67 high x 55 wide
Snowman finished design sizes:
28-count fabric – 4¾ x 4 inches
22-count fabric – 6 x 5 inches
36-count fabric – 3¾ x 3 inches

Bear Gift Bag

Santa Gift Bag

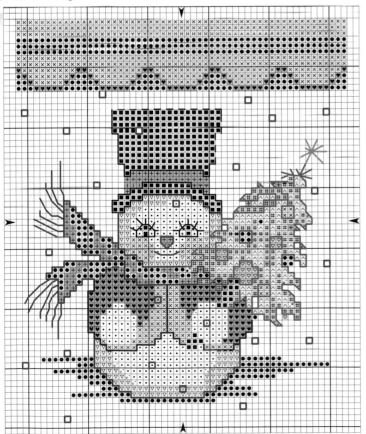

Snowman Gift Bag

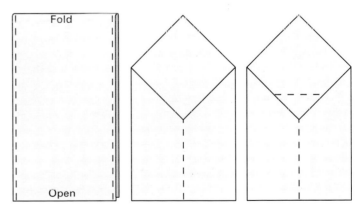

Fold

Open

Diagram for Bag Construction

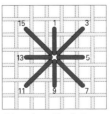

Algerian Eyelet

A STORY
to Stitch

O, Holy Night—the stars are brightly shining. It is the night of our Dear Savior's birth. Create a wonderful heirloom and begin a new family tradition. This year, stitch the Holy Family to proudly display in your home, then each year following, add one or two figures until you complete the entire Nativity.

Grace your home with a majestic manger scene that spreads the Good News.

Here, the beautifully matted and framed Holy Family shows the Christ Child, wrapped in swaddling clothes, resting on His mother's lap.

Separately stitched humble shepherds and wise men clad in lustruous robes pay homage to the Newborn King, while the animals of the fields are nearby. A gloriously radiant angel in a lovely lavender gown keeps watch over the entire heavenly scene while playing a gold-stringed harp. All were designed by Lorri Birmingham from Granby, Connecticut, for stitching on 28-count Jobelan fabric.

THE CHRISTMAS *Story*

nd it came to pass in those days, that there went out a decree from Caesar Augustus, that all the world should be taxed. And this taxing was first made when Cyrenius was governor of Syria. And all went to be taxed, every one into his own city.

And Joseph also went up from Galilee, out of the city of Nazareth into Judea, unto the city of David, which is called Bethlehem (because he was of the house and lineage of David), to be taxed with Mary his espoused wife, being great with child.

And so it was, that, while they were there, the days were accomplished that she should be delivered. And she brought forth her firstborn Son, wrapped Him in swaddling clothes, and laid Him in a manger; because there was no room for them in the inn.

And there were in the same country shepherds abiding in the field, keeping watch over their flock by night. And, lo, the angel of the Lord came upon them, and the glory of the Lord shone about them; and they were sore afraid.

And the angel said unto them, Fear not: for, behold, I bring you good tidings of great joy, which shall be to all people. For unto you is born this day in the city of David a Saviour, which is Christ the Lord.

And this shall be a sign unto you; Ye shall find the Babe wrapped in swaddling clothes, lying in a manger.

And suddenly there was with the angel a multitude of the heavenly host praising God, and saying: Glory to God in the highest, and on Earth peace, good will toward men.

And it came to pass, as the angels were gone away from them into heaven, the shepherds said to one another, Let us now go even unto Bethlehem, and see this thing which is come to pass, which the Lord hath made known unto us.

And they came with haste, and found Mary and Joseph, and the Babe lying in a manger. And when they had seen it, they made known abroad the saying which was told them concerning this child. And all they that heard it wondered at those things which were told them by the shepherds.

But Mary kept all these things, and pondered them in her heart. And the shepherds returned, glorifying and praising God for all the things that they had heard and seen, as it was told unto them.

From Luke 2:1-20, King James version of the Bible

NATIVITY

As shown on pages 32-33.

Fabric and Threads

For the family
18×18" piece of 28-count antique white Jobelan fabric
For the kings, shepherds, and angel
Six 14×10" pieces of 28-count antique white Jobelan fabric
Six 12×9" pieces *each* of polyester fleece and coordinating print cotton fabric
For the sheep
Two 6×6" pieces of 28-count antique white Jobelan fabric
Two 6×6" pieces *each* of polyester fleece and coordinating print cotton fabric
For all pieces
Cotton embroidery floss in colors listed in keys on *pages 36-49*
One additional skein *each* of DMC 000, 415, 434, 931, and 3371
Blending filament in colors listed in keys on *pages 40-44*
Two spools of Kreinik 221 antique gold #8 braid

Supplies

Needle
Embroidery hoop
Air-soluble fabric-marking pen
Tracing paper
Lightweight cardboard
Crafts glue
Matching sewing thread
Polyester fiberfill
For each standing figure
22" to 30" piece of ¼" to ¾"-wide flat braid trim in desired colors
Desired frame and mat (we used a 19×19×3"-deep frame and lined the inside of the frame with a light green suede mat)

Instructions

Zigzag-stitch or overcast the edges of each piece of the Jobelan fabric to prevent fraying. Find the center of the desired chart and the center of the appropriate piece of fabric.

Use three plies of floss or one strand of braid to work the cross-stitches over two threads of the fabric. Work the blended-needle stitches using two plies of floss and two strands of filament. Work the half cross-stitches using two plies of floss in the direction of the symbol. Use one strand of braid to work the straight stitches. Use two plies of floss to work the French knots. Work the backstitches using one ply of floss.

For the figures, use the air-soluble fabric-marking pen to draw a simplified shape ½" beyond the outline of the stitched design. Baste the fleece to the stitched piece, sewing ½" beyond the cross-stitches. Cut out the fabric ½" beyond the marked line. Using the stitched piece as a pattern, cut a matching back from the calico fabric.

Sew the front and back of each figure together along the basting lines, leaving the bottom edge open. Clip the curves and turn right side out. Stuff firmly with the polyester fiberfill. Turn the raw edges under ¼".

For the base, trace the appropriate base pattern onto the tracing paper and cut out. Transfer the oval to the cardboard; cut out. From the cotton fabric, cut an oval ½" larger than the cardboard. Center and glue the cardboard oval to the wrong side of the fabric oval.

Fold the raw edges to the back; glue, clipping as needed. Allow the glue to dry. Hand-stitch the base to the bottom of the figure. Glue the braid over the side seam lines.

Stitch the framed piece in the same manner as the figures. Press the finished stitchery from the back. Mat and frame the piece as desired.

Sheep Base

Sheep #1

Sheep #1 stitch count: *38 high x 40 wide*
Sheep #1 finished design sizes:
28-count fabric – 2¾ x 2⅞ inches
22-count fabric – 3½ x 3⅝ inches
36-count fabric – 2⅛ x 2¼ inches

Sheep #2

Sheep #2 stitch count: *41 high x 37 wide*
Sheep #2 finished design sizes:
28-count fabric – 3 x 2⅝ inches
22-count fabric – 3¾ x 3⅜ inches
36-count fabric – 2¼ x 2⅛ inches

SHEEP

Anchor		DMC	
002	•	000	White
401	⋈	413	Pewter
235	#	414	Steel
398	△	415	Pearl gray

HALF-CROSS STITCH
(stitch in direction of symbol)

886	╱	3047	Yellow beige

BACKSTITCH

382	╱	3371	Black brown– all stitches

FRENCH KNOT

382	•	3371	Black brown– sheep's eyes

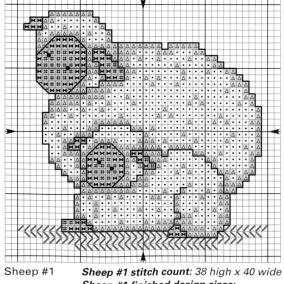

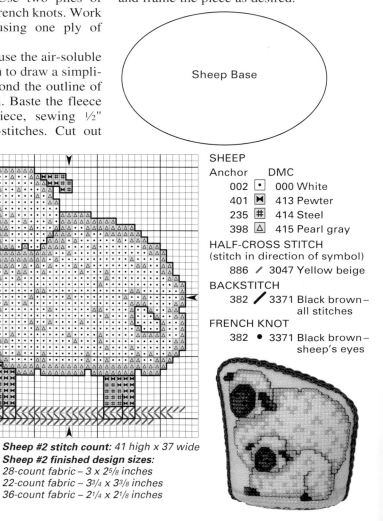

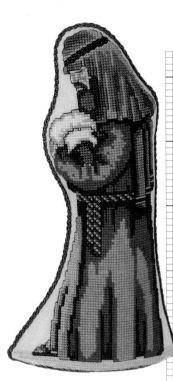

STANDING SHEPHERD

Anchor		DMC	
002	•	000	White
100	◉	327	Antique violet
1014	◆	355	Deep terra cotta
5975	✕	356	Medium terra cotta
401	⋈	413	Pewter
235	#	414	Steel
398	△	415	Pearl gray
358	♠	433	Dark chestnut
1046	=	435	Light chestnut
267	⊠	469	Avocado
882	—	758	Light terra cotta
1021	♡	761	Salmon
277	✳	830	Dark bronze
907	▽	832	Medium bronze
945	I	834	Pale bronze
1035	●	930	Dark antique blue
1033	+	932	True antique blue
269	▲	936	Pine green
881	╱	945	Dark ivory
1010	⊐	951	Medium ivory
261	∿	3053	Gray green
1032	◇	3752	Light antique blue
1008	◯	3773	Rose beige

HALF-CROSS STITCH
(stitch in direction of symbol)
886 ╱ 3047 Yellow beige

BACKSTITCH
382 ╱ 3371 Black brown—
all stitches

Stitch count: 135 high x 77 wide
Finished design sizes:
28-count fabric – 9⅝ x 5½ inches
22-count fabric – 12¼ x 7 inches
36-count fabric – 7½ x 4¼ inches

Standing Shepherd

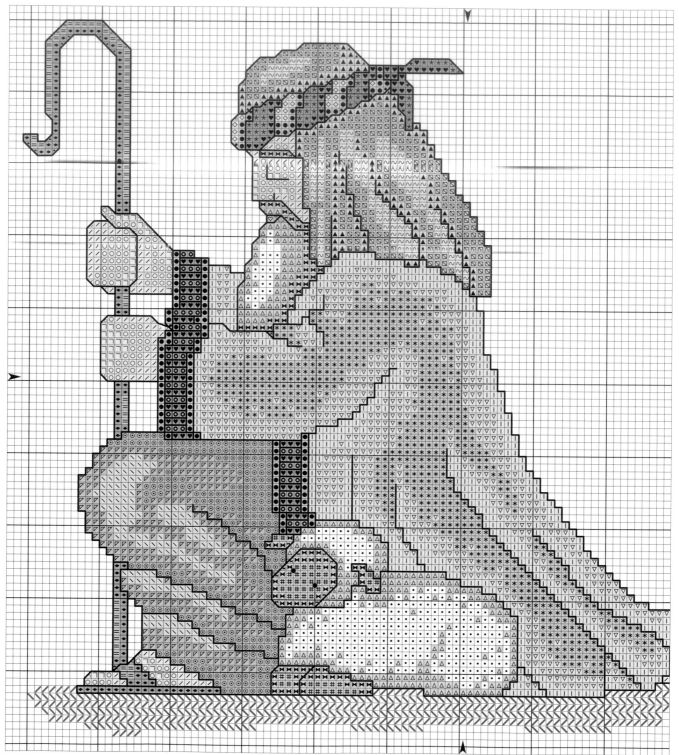

Kneeling Shepherd

Anchor		DMC		Anchor		DMC		Anchor		DMC
002	·	000 White		277	✳	830 Dark bronze		1027	✶	3722 True shell pink
897	♥	221 Deep shell pink		907	▽	832 Medium bronze		1008	◯	3773 Rose beige
100	⊙	327 Antique violet		945	I	834 Pale bronze		1050	◉	3781 Dark mocha
401	⋈	413 Pewter		1035	●	930 Antique blue				
235	⊞	414 Steel		269	▲	936 Pine green		**HALF-CROSS STITCH**		
398	△	415 Pearl gray		881	╱	945 Dark ivory		(stitch in direction of symbol)		
358	◆	433 Dark chestnut		1010	⊐	951 Medium ivory		886	╱	3047 Yellow beige
1046	═	435 Light chestnut		903	◹	3032 Medium mocha		**BACKSTITCH**		
267	◨	469 Avocado		903	◺	3033 Pale mocha		382	╱	3371 Black brown –
1021	♡	761 Salmon		261	∾	3053 Gray green				all stitches
								FRENCH KNOT		
								382	●	3371 Black brown –
										sheep's eyes

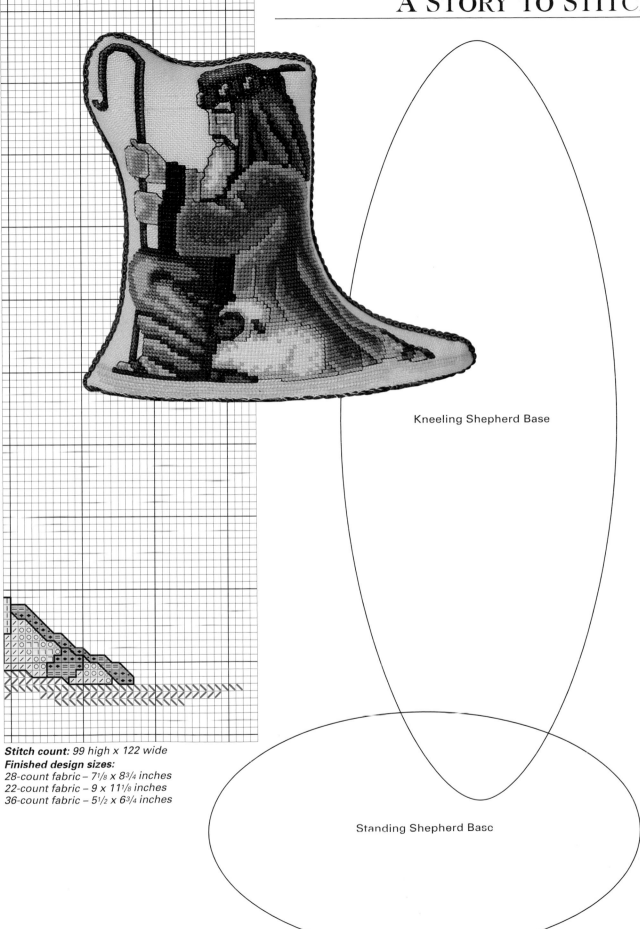

Stitch count: *99 high x 122 wide*
Finished design sizes:
28-count fabric – 7¹/₈ x 8³/₄ inches
22-count fabric – 9 x 11¹/₈ inches
36-count fabric – 5¹/₂ x 6³/₄ inches

Kneeling Shepherd Base

Standing Shepherd Base

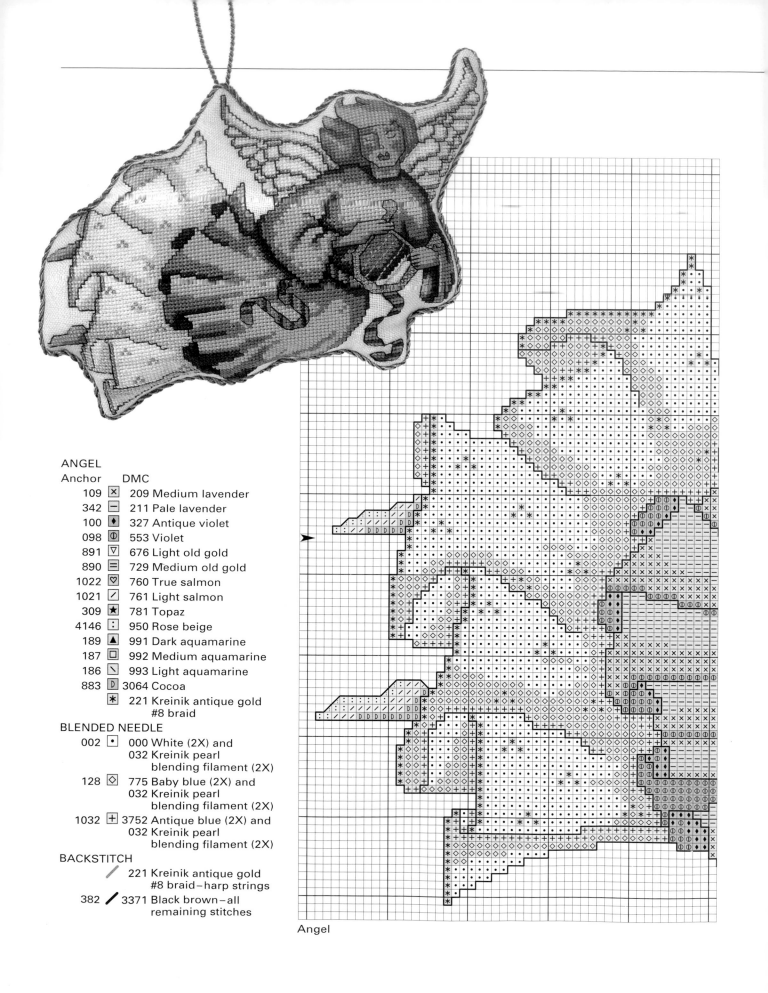

ANGEL

Anchor		DMC	
109	☒	209	Medium lavender
342	▬	211	Pale lavender
100	◆	327	Antique violet
098	◍	553	Violet
891	▽	676	Light old gold
890	▤	729	Medium old gold
1022	♡	760	True salmon
1021	⁄	761	Light salmon
309	★	781	Topaz
4146	⋮	950	Rose beige
189	▲	991	Dark aquamarine
187	▫	992	Medium aquamarine
186	◿	993	Light aquamarine
883	D	3064	Cocoa
	✳	221	Kreinik antique gold #8 braid

BLENDED NEEDLE

002	⊡	000 White (2X) and 032 Kreinik pearl blending filament (2X)
128	◈	775 Baby blue (2X) and 032 Kreinik pearl blending filament (2X)
1032	⊞	3752 Antique blue (2X) and 032 Kreinik pearl blending filament (2X)

BACKSTITCH

	⁄	221 Kreinik antique gold #8 braid—harp strings
382	╱	3371 Black brown—all remaining stitches

Angel

Stitch count: 91 high x 128 wide
Finished design sizes:
28-count fabric – 6½ x 9¼ inches
22-count fabric – 8¼ x 11⅝ inches
36-count fabric – 5⅛ x 7⅛ inches

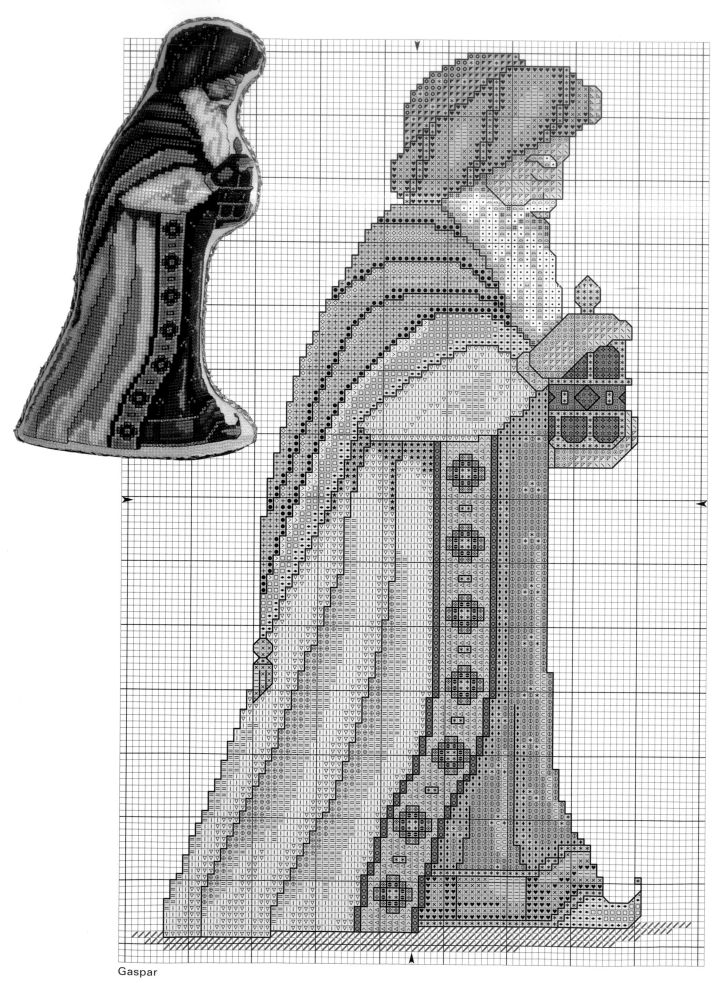

Gaspar

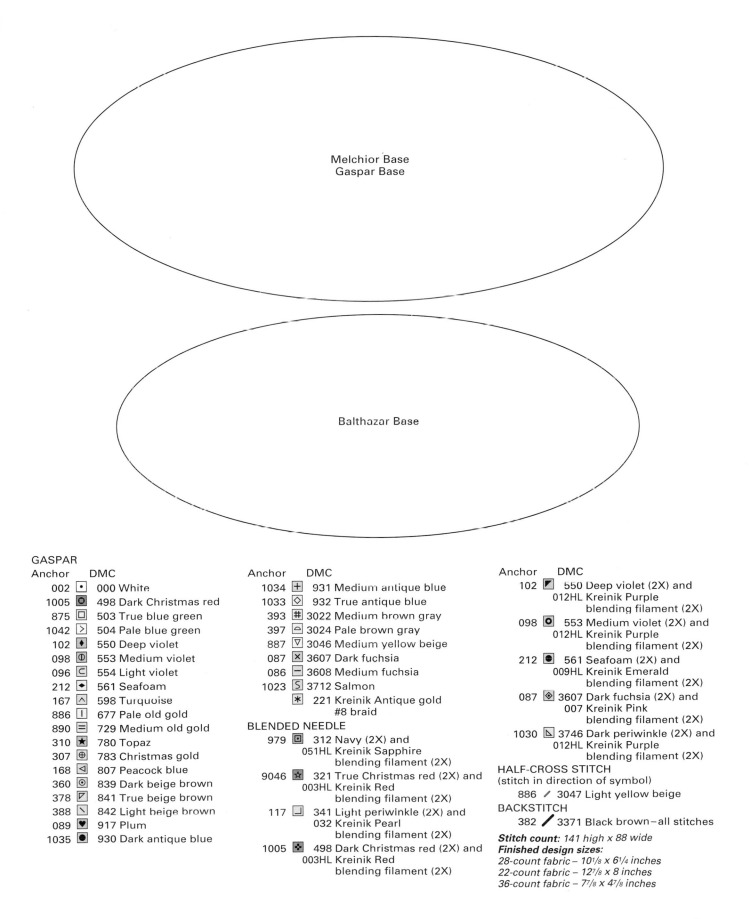

Melchior Base
Gaspar Base

Balthazar Base

GASPAR

Anchor		DMC
002	·	000 White
1005	◘	498 Dark Christmas red
875	□	503 True blue green
1042	▷	504 Pale blue green
102	◆	550 Deep violet
098	⬓	553 Medium violet
096	C	554 Light violet
212	◆	561 Seafoam
167	∧	598 Turquoise
886	I	677 Pale old gold
890	=	729 Medium old gold
310	★	780 Topaz
307	⊕	783 Christmas gold
168	◁	807 Peacock blue
360	◉	839 Dark beige brown
378	▽	841 True beige brown
388	◺	842 Light beige brown
089	♥	917 Plum
1035	●	930 Dark antique blue

Anchor		DMC
1034	+	931 Medium antique blue
1033	◇	932 True antique blue
393	⊞	3022 Medium brown gray
397	⬒	3024 Pale brown gray
887	▽	3046 Medium yellow beige
087	✗	3607 Dark fuchsia
086	−	3608 Medium fuchsia
1023	S	3712 Salmon
	✳	221 Kreinik Antique gold #8 braid

BLENDED NEEDLE

Anchor		DMC
979	▣	312 Navy (2X) and 051HL Kreinik Sapphire blending filament (2X)
9046	☆	321 True Christmas red (2X) and 003HL Kreinik Red blending filament (2X)
117	⌐	341 Light periwinkle (2X) and 032 Kreinik Pearl blending filament (2X)
1005	✜	498 Dark Christmas red (2X) and 003HL Kreinik Red blending filament (2X)

Anchor		DMC
102	◪	550 Deep violet (2X) and 012HL Kreinik Purple blending filament (2X)
098	◉	553 Medium violet (2X) and 012HL Kreinik Purple blending filament (2X)
212	●	561 Seafoam (2X) and 009HL Kreinik Emerald blending filament (2X)
087	◈	3607 Dark fuchsia (2X) and 007 Kreinik Pink blending filament (2X)
1030	◺	3746 Dark periwinkle (2X) and 012HL Kreinik Purple blending filament (2X)

HALF-CROSS STITCH
(stitch in direction of symbol)

886	╱	3047 Light yellow beige

BACKSTITCH

382	╱	3371 Black brown–all stitches

Stitch count: 141 high x 88 wide
Finished design sizes:
28-count fabric – 10 1/8 x 6 1/4 inches
22-count fabric – 12 7/8 x 8 inches
36-count fabric – 7 7/8 x 4 7/8 inches

MELCHIOR AND BALTHAZAR

Anchor		DMC	
002	•	000	White
398	△	415	Pearl gray
895	U	223	Shell pink
862	▲	520	Olive drab
099	✣	552	Dark violet
890	=	729	Old gold
1021	♡	761	Salmon
310	★	780	Topaz
307	⊕	783	Christmas gold
132	◪	797	Royal blue
136	⌂	799	Medium Delft blue
144	▷	800	Pale Delft blue
089	♥	917	Plum
1035	●	930	Dark antique blue
1034	+	931	Medium antique blue
1033	◇	932	True antique blue
881	∠	945	Dark ivory
1010	⊐	951	Medium ivory
4146	:	950	Rose beige
887	▽	3046	Medium yellow beige
681	⊠	3051	Dark gray green
261	∿	3053	Light gray green

Anchor		DMC	
883	D	3064	Light cocoa
382	■	3371	Black brown
087	✕	3607	Fuchsia
086	−	3608	Medium fuchsia
1008	○	3773	Rose beige
1007	★	3772	Dark cocoa
	✳	221	Kreinik Antique gold #8 braid

BLENDED NEEDLE

Anchor		DMC	
110	▽	208	Dark lavender (2X) and 012 Kreinik Purple blending filament (2X)
109	▽	209	Medium lavender (2X) and 012 Kreinik Purple blending filament (2X)
342	L	211	Pale lavender (2X) and 012 Kreinik Purple blending filament (2X)
979	▣	312	Navy (2X) and 051HL Kreinik Sapphire blending filament (2X)
9046	★	321	Christmas red (2X) and 003HL Kreinik Purple blending filament (2X)

Anchor		DMC	
862	⊠	520	Olive drab (2X) and 009HL Kreinik Emerald blending filament (2X)
102	◪	550	Deep violet (2X) and 012HL Kreinik Purple blending filament (2X)
099	⊞	552	Dark violet (2X) and 012HL Kreinik Purple blending filament (2X)
098	◉	553	Medium violet (2X) and 012HL Kreinik Purple blending filament (2X)
212	⬟	561	Seafoam (2X) and 009HL Kreinik Emerald blending filament (2X)
132	▼	797	Royal blue (2X) and 051HL Kreinik Sapphire blending filament (2X)
136	‖	799	Delft blue (2X) and 051HL Kreinik Sapphire blending filament (2X)
089	▶	917	Plum (2X) and 007 Kreinik Pink blending filament (2X)

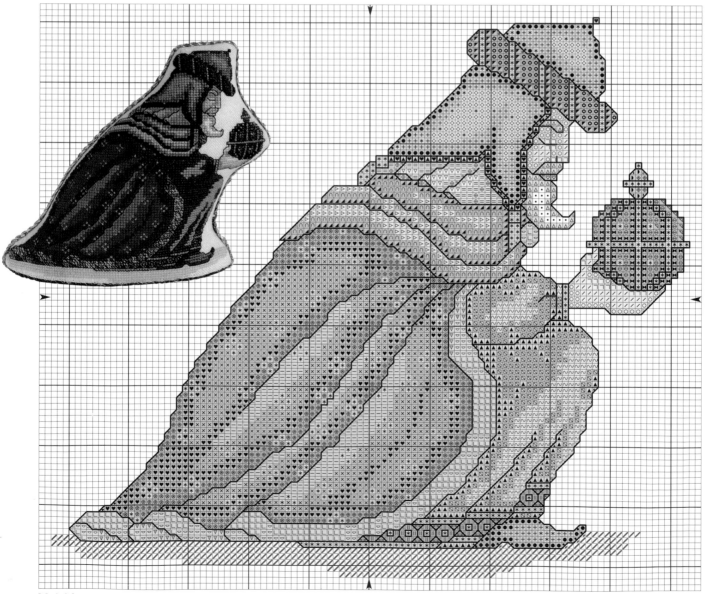

Melchior

A STORY TO STITCH

Anchor		DMC	
1035	⊞	930	Dark antique blue (2X) and
		051	Kreinik Sapphire blending filament (2X)
1034	⊖	931	Medium antique blue (2X) and
		051	Kreinik Sapphire blending filament (2X)
1033	◹	932	True antique blue (2X) and
		051	Kreinik Sapphire blending filament (2X)
087	◈	3607	Fuchsia (2X) and
		007	Kreinik Pink blending filament (2X)

HALF-CROSS STITCH
(stitch in direction of symbol)
886 ╱ 3047 Light yellow beige
BACKSTITCH
382 ╱ 3371 Black brown – all stitches

Balthazar Stitch count: 136 high x 97 wide
Balthazar Finished design sizes:
28-count fabric – 9³/₄ x 7 inches
22-count fabric – 12³/₈ x 8⁷/₈ inches
36-count fabric – 7¹/₂ x 5³/₈ inches

Melchior Stitch count: 93 high x 106 wide
Melchior Finished design sizes:
28-count fabric – 6⁵/₈ x 7¹/₂ inches
22-count fabric – 8¹/₂ x 9⁵/₈ inches
36-count fabric – 5¹/₈ x 5⁷/₈ inches

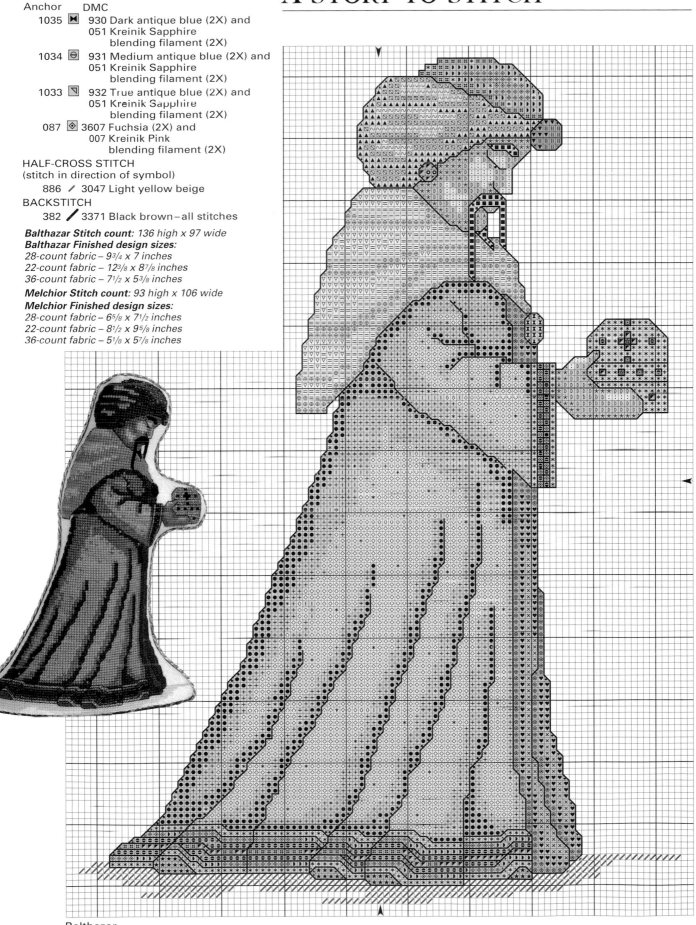

Balthazar

JOSEPH, MARY, BABY JESUS

Anchor		DMC
002	⊡	000 White
352	◆	300 Deep mahogany
1049	⊙	301 Medium mahogany
400	◑	317 True pewter
399	⊖	318 Light steel
119	◤	333 Deep periwinkle
118	⊘	340 Medium periwinkle
1025	✳	347 Deep salmon
1047	◲	402 Pale mahogany
914	◪	407 Medium cocoa
401	◫	413 Dark pewter
235	#	414 Dark steel
398	△	415 Pearl gray
358	▼	433 Dark chestnut
1046	✦	435 Light chestnut

Joseph, Mary, and Baby Jesus—Top Left

Anchor		DMC		Anchor		DMC		Anchor		DMC
875	□	503 True blue green		888	⊕	3045 Dark yellow beige		401	╱	413 Dark pewter
1042	▷	504 Pale blue green		887	▽	3046 Medium yellow beige		374	╱	420 Medium hazel
212	◆	561 Seafoam		059	✕	3350 Deep dusty rose		373	╱	422 Light hazel
936	◀	632 Deep cocoa		382	■	3371 Black brown		310	╱	434 Medium chestnut
886	Ⅱ	677 Pale old gold		1028	♥	3685 Mauve		380	╱	838 Deep beige brown
890	═	729 Medium old gold		1020	S	3713 Pale salmon		379	╱	840 Medium beige brown
1021	♡	761 Light salmon		075	▬	3733 Medium dusty rose				
128	◇	775 Baby blue		120	▷	3747 Pale periwinkle				
310	★	780 Topaz		1032	✚	3752 Antique blue				
177	●	792 Cornflower blue		779	⊠	3768 Gray blue				
851	▲	924 Deep gray blue		1007	✶	3772 Dark cocoa				
850	∼	926 Medium gray blue		1008	⊙	3773 Medium rose beige				
274	⌂	928 Pale gray blue								
881	⟋	945 Dark ivory								
4146	⫶	950 Light rose beige								
1010	⊐	951 Medium ivory								

BACKSTITCH

401 413 Dark pewter
374 420 Medium hazel
373 422 Light hazel
310 434 Medium chestnut
380 838 Deep beige brown
379 840 Medium beige brown

BACKSTITCH

382 ╱ 3371 Black brown –
all stitches

HALF-CROSS STITCH
(stitch in direction of symbol)

319 ╱ 318 Light steel
215 ╱ 320 Pistachio

Stitch count: 169 high x 203 wide
Finished design sizes:
28-count fabric – 12 1/8 x 14 1/2 inches
22-count fabric – 15 3/8 x 18 1/2 inches
36-count fabric – 9 3/8 x 11 1/4 inches

Joseph, Mary, and Baby Jesus—Top Right

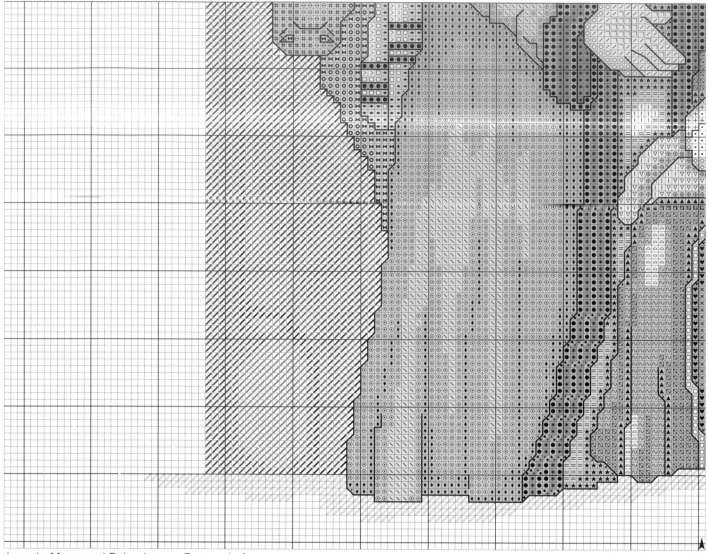

Joseph, Mary, and Baby Jesus—Bottom Left

JOSEPH, MARY, BABY JESUS

Anchor	DMC	
002	⊡	000 White
352	◆	300 Deep mahogany
1049	⊙	301 Medium mahogany
400	◙	317 True pewter
399	⊖	318 Light steel
119	◩	333 Deep periwinkle
118	⏀	340 Medium periwinkle
1025	✳	347 Deep salmon
1047	◣	402 Pale mahogany
914	◨	407 Medium cocoa
401	⋈	413 Dark pewter
235	⊞	414 Dark steel
398	△	415 Pearl gray
358	▼	433 Dark chestnut
1046	☆	435 Light chestnut

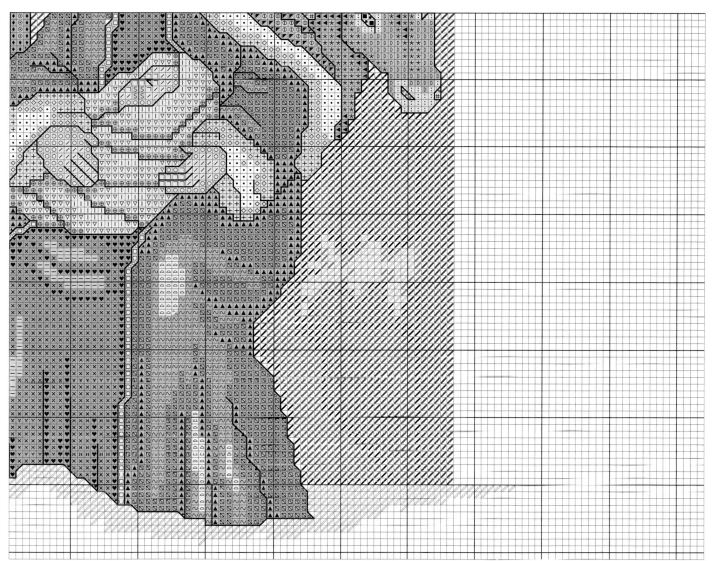

Joseph, Mary, and Baby Jesus—Bottom Right

Anchor		DMC	
875	□	503	True blue green
1042	▷	504	Pale blue green
212	◖	561	Seafoam
936	◀	632	Deep cocoa
886	I	677	Pale old gold
890	=	729	Medium old gold
1021	▽	761	Light salmon
128	◇	775	Baby blue
310	★	780	Topaz
177	●	792	Cornflower blue
851	▲	924	Deep gray blue
850	∿	926	Medium gray blue
274	⌐	928	Pale gray blue
881	⁄	945	Dark ivory
4146	⁞	950	Light rose beige
1010	⊓	951	Medium ivory

Anchor		DMC	
888	⊕	3045	Dark yellow beige
887	▽	3046	Medium yellow beige
059	✕	3350	Deep dusty rose
382	■	3371	Black brown
1028	♥	3685	Mauve
1020	S	3713	Pale salmon
075	⊟	3733	Medium dusty rose
120	▷	3747	Pale periwinkle
1032	+	3752	Antique blue
779	◨	3768	Gray blue
1007	✳	3772	Dark cocoa
1008	○	3773	Medium rose beige

HALF-CROSS STITCH
(stitch in direction of symbol)

319	⁄	318	Light steel
215	⁄	320	Pistachio

Anchor		DMC	
401	⁄	413	Dark pewter
374	⁄	420	Medium hazel
373	⁄	422	Light hazel
310	⁄	434	Medium chestnut
380	⁄	838	Deep beige brown
379	⁄	840	Medium beige brown

BACKSTITCH

382	⁄	3371	Black brown— all stitches

Stitch count: *169 high x 203 wide*
Finished design sizes:
28-count fabric – 12 1/8 x 14 1/2 inches
22-count fabric – 15 3/8 x 18 1/2 inches
36-count fabric – 9 3/8 x 11 1/4 inches

49

Country COMFORTS

Entice friends and family with gifts steeped in country flavor. The recipients' delight when they unwrap their packages will be a just reward for your stitching efforts. From a tree filled with toys to leaping deer to smiling snowmen, you'll find cozy country icons to warm your home and delight your friends. Celebrate the season country-style!

Plant a festively decorated dowel tree on Aida cloth for all to enjoy, now and many Christmases to come. Decorated with every letter of the alphabet, the timeless tree displays a treasure-chest array of ornaments. There are bright balls, a star, a gaily wrapped box, a soldier with one big shoe, a Santa and—of course—a candy cane. Jeff Julseth from St.Paul, Minnesota, tops the tree with a heartfelt Christmas wish: Peace on Earth.

COUNTRY COMFORTS

A cozy country kitchen is the spice of life. Make your kitchen inviting with frolicking snowmen on a placemat and napkin set. Or embellish a hand towel that's ready to dry a child's tiny wet hands after a rousing snowball fight with Dad. Ursula Michael from Colchester, Connecticut, designed three different happy snow guys in all

to stitch on purchased accessories for immediate use. To finish these stitcheries, all you need to do is press—and use!

The sampler, *right,* offers a cheery welcome to holiday guests. Hang it in an entry or wherever visitors gather in your home. The bellpull's design contains several motifs and

patterns that lend themselves to other projects as well. For example, use the house-and-tree segment for an ornament, or the alphabet as a border along the edge of child's placemat. Alice Okon from Missoula, Montana, stitched her design on 16-count linen banding especially designed with selvage side edges so that finishing takes no time at all.

ABCDEFG
HIJKLMNO
PQRSTUVW
XYZ
abcdefghi
jklmnopqr
stuvwxyz
1234567890

COUNTRY COMFORTS

Christmas just wouldn't be Christmas without an Aida-cloth stocking stitched by you to hang from the fireplace mantel. With a whimsical nod to the ubiquitous country-cow motif, designer Jim Williams from Roosevelt Island, New York, looked for greener pastures and went in an entirely new direction with this cat-and-mouse design. The graphic boldness of the black and white threads on a bright green background makes this sock suitable for any cat lover as well as a deserving youngster.

You know Dancer and Prancer, now meet the rest of Santa's sure-footed helpers. Designer Alice Okon from Missoula, Montana, placed two on her primary-color sampler of Heatherfield fabric and accented their symmetric placement with a gracefully curved Celtic knot. If a pillow is more your style, you can stitch the adaptation on 8-count Heatherfield fabric. Both stitcheries are edged in a crisp white snowflake border and either variation makes a perfect winter accent in your country-home decor.

COUNTRY CHRISTMAS SAMPLER

As shown on page 51.

Fabric and Floss
18×16" piece of 14-count Fiddler's Lite Aida cloth
Cotton embroidery floss in colors listed in key

Supplies
Needle
Embroidery hoop
Desired frame and mat

Instructions
Zigzag-stitch or overcast the edges of the fabric to prevent fraying. Locate the center of the chart and the center of the fabric, begin stitching there. Use three plies of floss to work the cross-stitches. Work the French knots using one ply of the floss. Work the backstitches using one ply of the floss. Press the finished stitchery from the back. Mat and frame the piece as desired.

SNOWMAN HOSTESS SET

As shown on page 52.

Fabric and Floss
For each place mat
Purchased 13×18" 14-count royal blue Royal Classic place mat
For each napkin
Purchased 15×15" 14-count royal blue Royal Classic napkin
One additional skein of white floss (DMC 000)
For each towel
Purchased antique-blue towel with a 3"-wide 14-count Aida cloth insert
For each napkin ring
5½" length of 2¼"-wide 14-count Aida banding with a white-and-blue edge
2¾×5½" piece each of blue print fabric and lightweight fusible interfacing
Matching sewing thread

For all projects
Cotton embroidery floss in colors listed in key *on page 58*

Supplies
Needle

Instructions
For the place mat, count six squares from the edges on the lower left corner of the place mat; begin stitching the bottom row of the large snowman there. Use three plies of floss to work the cross-stitches. Work the backstitches using one ply of floss. Carefully press the finished stitchery from the back.

For the napkins, count six squares from the bottom and 10 squares from the left edge; begin stitching the medium snowman there. Use three plies of floss to work the cross-stitches. Work the backstitches using one ply of floss. Press the finished stitchery from the back.

For the towel, locate the center of small snowman chart and center of Aida cloth insert; begin stitching there. Use three plies of floss to work the cross-stitches. Work the backstitches using one ply of floss. Stitch four more snowman motifs, separating the bottom row of each snowman motif with 22 squares. Carefully press the finished towel from the back.

For the napkin rings, locate the center of the small snowman chart and the Aida banding; begin stitching there. Use three plies of floss to work the cross-stitches. Work the backstitches using one ply of floss.

Fuse the interfacing to the back of the print fabric following the manufacturer's instructions. With right sides together, sew the Aida banding to the print fabric, sewing very close along the finished edge of the banding fabric. Trim the print fabric to ¼" beyond the seam. Turn right side out; press. Slip-stitch the short edge closed. Overlap the short ends and hand-stitch together to form a ring.

COUNTRY CHRISTMAS SAMPLER

Anchor		DMC
002	•	000 White
042	+	309 Rose
399	I	318 Steel
100	▲	327 Antique violet
374	#	420 Medium hazel
162	*	517 Wedgwood blue
098	◇	553 Violet
295	☆	726 Topaz
1022	∕	760 Salmon
1005	▦	816 Garnet
944	●	869 Dark hazel
230	∧	909 Dark emerald
205	O	911 Medium emerald
881	X	945 Ivory
1001	△	976 Golden brown
187	▤	992 Medium aquamarine
928	▢	3761 Sky blue
188	♡	3814 True aquamarine
306	◉	3820 Straw

BACKSTITCH
002 / 000 White – gingerbread man, Jack-in-the-box
169 / 806 Peacock blue – angel's wings, Santa's beard
1005 / 816 Garnet – lettering, candy cane, puppet, Santa's mouth, gingerbread man's mouth, ball ornament, Jack-in-the-box mouth, packages
306 / 3820 Straw – candle, jingle bells, Jack-in-the-box, nutcracker, puppet, star hanger
360 / 898 Coffee brown – all remaining backstitches

FRENCH KNOTS
002 • 000 White – gingerbread man
360 • 898 Coffee brown – all eyes, bear's nose, jingle bells

LAZY DAISY
1005 ♄ 816 Garnet – bow on sprig of holly by nutcracker

Stitch count: 120 high x 89 wide
Finished design sizes:
14-count fabric – 8⅝ x 6⅜ inches
11-count fabric – 11 x 8⅛ inches
18-count fabric – 6⅔ x 5 inches

Lazy Daisy

Country Christmas Sampler

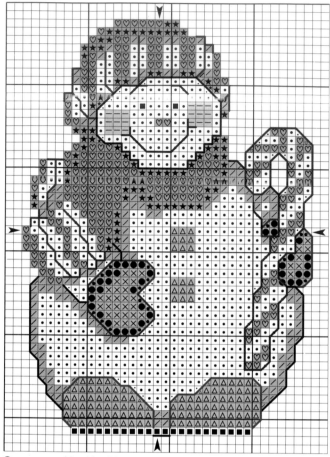

Snowman Napkin #1

Snowman Napkin #2

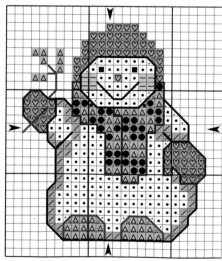

Snowman Towel and Napkin Ring

Snowman Hostess Set

Anchor		DMC	
002	•	000	White
1006	★	304	Christmas Red
403	■	310	Black
227	△	701	Christmas Green
131	●	798	Dark Delft Blue
130	✕	809	True Delft Blue
073	—	963	Rose Pink
869	╱	3743	Antique Violet
035	♡	3801	Watermelon

BACKSTITCH

1006	╱	304	Christmas Red – candycane, mittens, snowman hightlights
403	╱	310	Black – snowmen
227	╱	701	Christmas Green – mittens, snowboots
131	╱	798	Dark Delft Blue – mittens, hat, scarf

Snowman Napkin #1 stitch count: 50 high x 35 wide
Snowman Napkin #1 finished design size:
14-count fabric—3½ x 2½ inches
Snowman Napkin #2 stitch count: 41 high x 33 wide
Snowman Napkin #2 finished design size:
14-count fabric—2 x 2⅜ inches
Snowman Towel and Napkin Ring stitch count:
26 high x 22 wide
Snowman Towel and Napkin Ring finished
design size: 14-count fabric—1⅞ x 1½ inches

MINI SAMPLER

As shown on page 53.

Fabric and Floss

16" length of 4⅞"-wide 24-count red-on-raw-linen banding

Cotton embroidery floss in colors listed in the key

Kreinik 002 gold #8 braid

Supplies

Needle

Seed beads in colors listed in the key

Kreinik 003 red #8 braid

6¼"-long, ½"-diameter straight twig

Metallic gold spray paint

Hot-glue gun and hot-melt adhesive

Assorted star and moon charms

Instructions

Zigzag-stitch or overcast the ends of the banding to prevent fraying. Measure 4" from one end of the banding; begin stitching the top row of the chart there. Use three plies of floss to work the cross-stitches over two threads of the fabric. Work the running stitches using one strand of gold braid. Work the backstitches using one ply of floss. Attach the seed beads using one ply of matching floss. Trim the banding to measure 13". Place the stitchery facedown on a soft towel and press from the back; set aside. Spray the twig with the gold paint. Let the paint dry.

Turn up a ¼" hem twice on the bottom of the banding; hand-stitch in place. For the twig sleeve, press under ¼" at the top of the banding, then press under 1¼" of fabric. Whipstitch the pressed edge to the back of the banding. Insert the twig.

For the hanging cord, cut four 43" lengths each of the red and the gold #8 braid; combine into a single strand. Secure one end of the joined thread and twist; fold in half and allow the thread to twist together. Tie the ends of the twisted cord ½"-¾" from the ends of the twig. Use hot glue to secure the thread ends to the back of the cord, with the thread ends toward the center back of the twig.

Cut two 12" lengths each of red and gold braid. Join a length of red and gold thread together; fold in half to make a loop. Wrap the loop around the twisted cord near the twig, and slip the thread ends through the loop. Tie five charms to the threads at different levels. Trim the thread ends. The longest thread is 4"-long. Repeat on the other side.

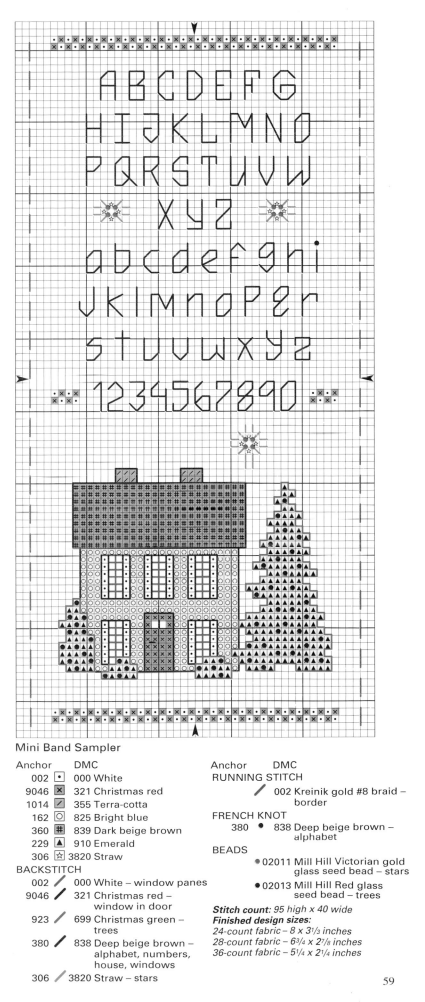

Mini Band Sampler

Anchor		DMC	
002	⊡	000	White
9046	⊠	321	Christmas red
1014	⊘	355	Terra-cotta
162	⊙	825	Bright blue
360	⊞	839	Dark beige brown
229	▲	910	Emerald
306	☆	3820	Straw

BACKSTITCH

002	╱	000	White – window panes
9046	╱	321	Christmas red – window in door
923	╱	699	Christmas green – trees
380	╱	838	Deep beige brown – alphabet, numbers, house, windows
306	╱	3820	Straw – stars

Anchor	DMC
RUNNING STITCH	
╱	002 Kreinik gold #8 braid – border
FRENCH KNOT	
380 ●	838 Deep beige brown – alphabet
BEADS	
●	02011 Mill Hill Victorian gold glass seed bead – stars
●	02013 Mill Hill Red glass seed bead – trees

Stitch count: 95 high x 40 wide

Finished design sizes:

24-count fabric – 8 x 3⅓ inches

28-count fabric – 6¾ x 2⅞ inches

36-count fabric – 5¼ x 2¼ inches

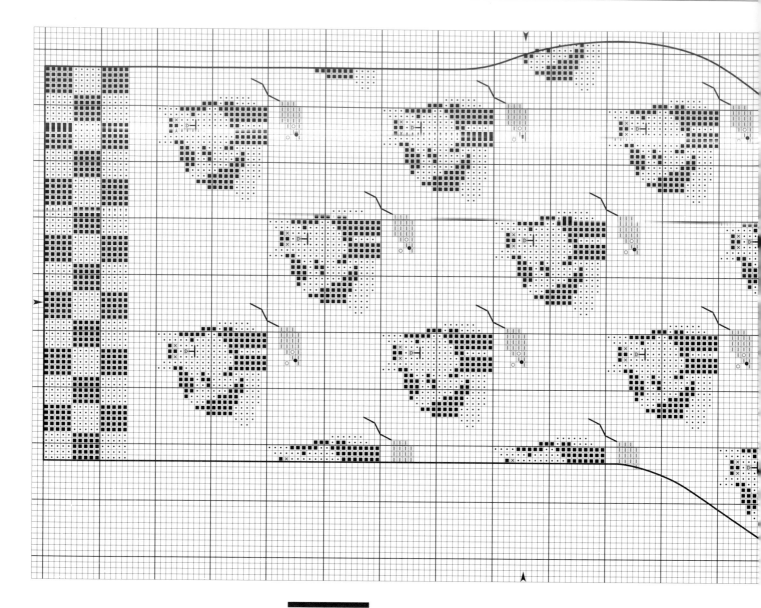

CAT AND MOUSE STOCKING

As shown on page 54, finished stocking is 17"-tall.

Fabric and Floss
24×18" piece of 11-count Christmas green Pearl Aida cloth
12×18" piece of fusible fleece
½ yard of 45"-wide black-and-white gingham fabric
Cotton embroidery floss in colors listed in key

Supplies
Needle; embroidery hoop
Seed beads in colors listed in key
Air-soluble fabric marker

1½ yards of ¼"-diameter purchased black sew-in piping
Matching sewing thread
45" length of 2½"- wide white flat eyelet lace
4½ yards of ½"-wide black-and-white striped ribbon
Four ½"-diameter pom-poms
Crafts glue

Instructions
Zigzag-stitch or overcast the edges of the Aida cloth to prevent fraying. Measure 3" from the edges on the top right corner of the fabric; begin stitching the first row of the chart there. Use four plies of floss to work the cross-stitches. Use one ply of floss to work the French knots. Work the straight stitches using two plies

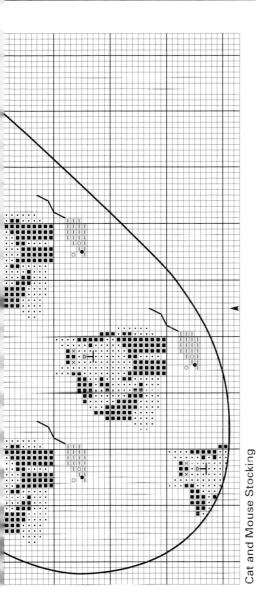

Cat and Mouse Stocking

of floss. Attach the seed beads with sewing thread.

Use the air-soluble marker to draw the stocking outline. Fuse the fleece to the back of the fabric. Cut out ¼" beyond the marker line. Use the fabric stocking as a pattern to cut one back and two lining pieces from the gingham fabric.

Baste the piping along the sides and the foot of the stocking with raw edges even. Sew the stocking front to the back, right sides together, along the basting lines. Leave the top edge open. Baste the piping along the entire top of the stocking with raw edges even.

Sew the short ends of the lace together to form a continuous loop. Run a gathering thread ⅜" from the

raw edge of the loop. Pull the threads to fit the perimeter of the stocking top; adjust the gathers evenly. Sew the lace ruffle to the stocking along the piping stitching line.

Sew the lining pieces together, right sides facing, leaving the top open and and leaving an opening at the bottom of the foot; *do not* turn. With right sides together, slip the stocking inside the lining. Stitch the stocking to the lining at the top edge; turn the stocking right side out. Slip-stitch the opening closed. Tuck the lining into the stocking; press.

Cut one each 4", 5", 6", and 7" length from the striped ribbon. Glue a pom-pom to one end of each ribbon. Tack the opposite end of each ribbon to the top right corner of the stocking. Make a 24-loop bow from the remaining ribbon; thoroughly secure the layers at the center of the bow. Tack the bow to the top right corner of the stocking.

WINTER WONDERLAND SAMPLER

As shown on page 55.

Fabric and Floss
20×16" piece of 26-count navy Heatherfield fabric
Cotton embroidery floss in colors listed in key on *page 63*

Supplies
Needle; embroidery hoop
Desired frame and mat

Instructions
Zigzag-stitch or overcast the edges of the fabric to prevent fraying. Measure 4" from the edges on one corner of the fabric; begin the border there. Use three plies of floss to work the cross-stitches over two threads of the fabric. Work the straight stitches using two plies of floss. Work the backstitches using one ply of floss unless otherwise specified in the key. Press the finished stitchery from the back. Mat and frame the piece as desired.

WINTER WONDERLAND PILLOW

As shown on page 55.

Fabric and Floss
22×22" piece of 8-count navy Heatherfield fabric
1½ yards of red-and-green plaid fabric
14½×14½" piece of navy fabric
Cotton embroidery floss in colors listed in key on *page 63*

Supplies
Needle; embroidery hoop
Matching sewing thread
Polyester fiberfill

Instructions
Zigzag-stitch or overcast the edges of the fabric to prevent fraying. Locate the center of the chart and the center of the fabric; begin stitching six threads from this point. Use six plies of floss to work the cross-stitches over one thread of the fabric. Work the straight stitches using two plies of floss. Work the backstitches using two plies of floss.

Trim the Heatherfield fabric ¾" beyond the outside of the stitched border. Baste the navy fabric to the wrong side of the stitchery. From plaid fabric, cut a 14½×14¾" pillow back and two 7×70" bias ruffle strips. All measurements include ½-inch seam allowances.

Sew the short ends of the ruffle strips together, right sides facing, to form a continuous loop. Fold the loop in half lengthwise, with wrong sides together. Sew two lines of gathering threads ⅜" and ¼" from the raw edges of the loop. Pull the gathering threads to fit the perimeter of the pillow front. Adjust the gathers evenly; sew through all layers ½" from the edge of the fabric.

Sew the pillow front to the back, right sides together. Leave an opening for turning. Trim the seam allowances, clip corners, and turn right side out. Press carefully. Stuff the pillow firmly with fiberfill and slipstitch the opening closed.

Winter Wonderland Sampler

Winter Wonderland Pillow

WINTER WONDERLAND SAMPLER AND PILLOW

Anchor		DMC
387	•	Ecru
403	■	310 Black
9046	✕	321 Christmas red
890	+	729 Old gold
380	◆	838 Deep beige brown
379	☆	840 Medium beige brown
229	○	910 Emerald
373	△	3828 Hazel

Anchor		DMC
BACKSTITCH		
9046	╱	321 Christmas red – lettering (2X)
380	╱	838 Deep beige brown – deer, knot (1X)
STRAIGHT STITCH		
387	╱	Ecru – snowflakes (2X)

Sampler stitch count: 158 high x 111 wide
Sampler finished design sizes:
26-count fabric – 12¼ x 8½ inches
22-count fabric – 14³⁄₈ x 10¹⁄₈ inches
36-count fabric – 8³⁄₄ x 6¹⁄₄ inches

Pillow stitch count: 111 high x 111 wide
Pillow finished design size:
8-count fabric – 13⁷⁄₈ x 13⁷⁄₈ inches

DECK THE Boughs

At Christmas, visions of Santa, stars and snowflakes, and elves and nutcrackers come to mind as easily as poetic sugarplums. Adorn your tree with an enchanting assortment of holiday trims and treasures to share the sentiments of the season. Choose from an array of ornaments featuring greetings, symbols of the season, fun-loving elves, and elegant beaded snowflake swirls.

Welcome friends and family with festive greetings and seasonal symbols stitched on scraps of perforated paper. Alice Okon from Missoula, Montana, designed five favorite holiday images—a Christmas treasure chest, a New Year's gift, a decorative tree, beribboned candles, and a colorful heart—that work up quickly in miniature for use as ornaments on the tree, package gift tags, or as inserts in purchased greeting cards with matching envelopes.

DECK THE BOUGHS

Joyful elves help Santa Claus put the finishing touches on festive decorations and toys. One cuts out stars for an evergreen's garland, the second pulls sugary confection into a barber-pole candy cane, and the third paints finishing touches on a train. The smiling threesome is clad in darling outfits, and all merrily pose for their picture on 18-count Aida cloth. Designer Penny Duff from Kennebunk, Maine, kept the little guys fairly simple so you can mix and match colors of your choice for an endless variety. What a great project to use up lots of leftover lengths of floss!

DECK THE BOUGHS

When the clock is running out and the hour is late—relax. You can create a fabulous tree full of starry trimmings like the ones shown here in less time than you've ever imagined. Virginia Soskin from Ormond Beach, Florida, designed these beaded stars so they'd be easy enough to make by the dozen.

Glistening metallic perforated paper and glass seed beads in ice-crystal-like hues provide galactic glints to these sparkly ornaments.

Create a trio of tumbling elves to climb up your tree, simply by using chenille stems and stitched perforated-paper bodies, hands, and feet. They're delightfully easy to create and as fun to make as they are to give. Project designer Ruth Schmuff from Randallstown, Maryland, kept finishing chores to a minumum—just cut out, glue, and hang. With time to spare, you'll even be able to make some of the other ornaments in this chapter!

Midnight strikes and the magic starts. Clara is in for a spectacular adventure, ending, of course, in the transformation of the nutcracker into a handsome prince. Our cross-stitch version is dapperly dressed in bright blue and gold and works up beautifully on 28-count Monaco fabric. Designer Mary Kay Werning from Des Moines, Iowa, added glittering metallic threads and cranberry-color beads to make this nutcracker a jeweled work of art.

Beautiful embroidery was a hallmark of Victorian needlework. Designer Sandy Orton from Rodeo, California, recaptured the romance of a bygone era when gracious stitches were considered an art. These embroidered and embellished baubles are done in shimmering Christmas colors that contrast nicely against the 30-count white Murano fabric. Glimmering thread and tassels make the ornaments sparkle.

Country Christmas Cards & Tags

As shown on pages 64 and 65.

Fabric and Thread

For each card or tag

6×5" piece of 14-count white
  perforated paper
Cotton embroidery floss in colors
  listed in the key
Kreinik 002 gold #8 braid

Supplies

Needle
Red and gold seed beads
Crafts glue

For the gift tags

Kreinik 002P gold cable
3¼×4½" piece of white felt
5×3½" piece of burgundy felt
5½×4" piece of green felt
13" length of ⅛"-wide metallic
  gold flat trim
10" length of ¹⁄₁₆"-diameter
  metallic gold cord

For the cards

Purchased 5½×3¾" white card
  with a 4×2½" opening
Kreinik 002P gold cable
Delta Ceramcoat acrylic paints:
  2056 Berry red and
  2421 Jubilee green
Metallic gold paint
Sponge
Masking tape

Instructions

For the cards or gift tags: Find the center of the desired chart and the center of one piece of perforated paper; begin stitching there. Use three plies of floss or one strand of braid to work the cross-stitches. Work the backstitches using one ply of floss unless otherwise specified in the key. Attach the seed beads using one ply of matching floss.

For the gift tags: For the tassel, cut two 6" lengths of medium old gold (DMC 729); set aside. Cut fifteen 2"-long strands each of medium old gold (DMC 729) and gold cable. Join the strands forming a bundle.

Tie the center of the bundle with one 6" length of floss. Holding the thread bundle in one hand, tightly wrap the remaining 6" length of floss around the bundle ⅛" from the tied end. Trim the tassel to measure ½"-long. Thread the ends of the first 6" length of floss into a needle. Sew through the front of the tag and secure the threads at the back.

Cover the wrong side of the design with glue. Center the design atop the white felt. Trim one square beyond the stitched area as shown on the chart. Center and glue the design atop the burgundy felt. Cut out a scant ⅛" beyond the white felt. Repeat with the green felt, cutting out a scant ⅛" beyond the burgundy felt. Glue the gold trim around the outer edges of the perforated paper. Use a paper punch to make a hole in the top center of the tag. Insert the gold cord through the hole; knot the cord ends.

For the cards: Use the sponge to paint the frame area of the card with the red or green acrylic paint. Let the paint dry. Dip the sponge into the metallic gold paint. Blot the excess paint onto a paper towel. Randomly dab the gold paint onto the frame. Let the paint dry. Centering the design within the card opening, tape the stitchery to the inside of the card.

Elf Ornaments

As shown on pages 66 and 67, the finished ornaments are 4" tall.

Fabric and Floss

For each ornament

6×4" piece of 18-count ivory Aida
  cloth
4×3¼" piece of 18-count ivory
  Aida cloth
Cotton embroidery floss in colors
  listed in the key on *page 74*

Supplies

Needle
Polyester fiberfill
Metallic gold sewing thread

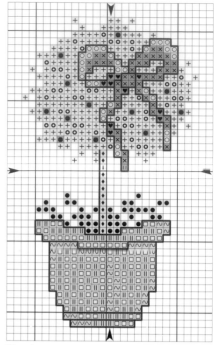

Topiary

**COUNTRY CHRISTMAS CARDS
AND ORNAMENTS**

Anchor		DMC	
002	·	000	White
042	○	309	Rose
1045	□	436	Tan
1005	☒	498	Christmas red
858	▽	524	Olive drab
936	◆	632	Cocoa
891	⑤	676	Light old gold
886	▬	677	Pale old gold
890	‖	729	Medium old gold
301	⊕	744	Yellow
024	♡	776	Pink
310	~	780	Topaz
043	♥	815	Garnet
244	◎	987	Medium forest green
242	✛	989	Pale forest green
903	●	3032	Mocha
260	⊓	3364	Loden
076	▲	3731	Dark dusty rose
075	△	3733	Medium dusty rose
	✳	002	Kreinik gold #8 braid

BACKSTITCH

246	╱	986	Dark forest green – candles (1X)
382	╱	3371	Black-brown – lettering (2X)
	╱	002	Kreinik gold #8 braid – bottle (1X)
382	╱	3371	Black-brown – all remaining stitches (1X)

LAZY DAISY

246	⟋	986	Dark forest green – candles (1X)

SEED BEADS

	●	02011	Mill Hill Victorian gold – heart
	●	02012	Mill Hill Royal plum – topiary and New Year

TASSEL

890	☒	729	Medium old gold and 002P Kreinik gold cable

Continued

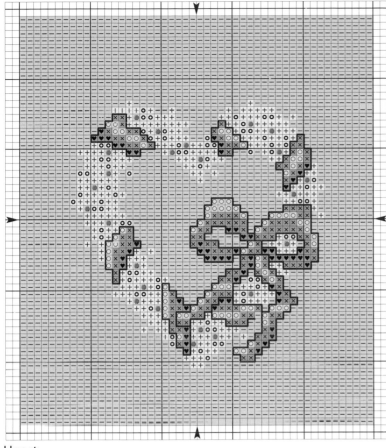

Heart

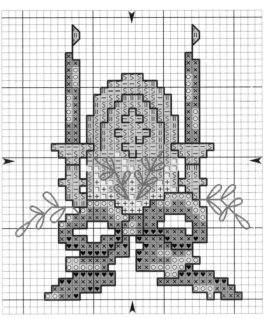

Candles

Happy New Year

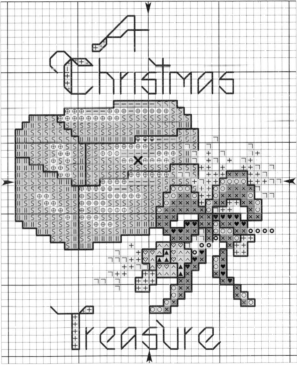

Christmas Treasure

Numbers Chart

Candles stitch count: 39 high x 33 wide
Candles finished design size:
14-count paper– 2³⁄₄ x 2³⁄₈ inches
Topiary stitch count: 44 high x 25 wide
Topiary finished design size:
14-count paper– 3¹⁄₄ x 1³⁄₄ inches

Heart stitch count: 58 high x 50 wide
Heart finished design size:
14-count paper– 4¹⁄₄ x 3¹⁄₂ inches
New Year stitch count: 43 high x 40 wide
New Year finished design size:
14-count paper– 3¹⁄₈ x 2⁷⁄₈ inches
Treasure stitch count: 47 high x 38 wide
Treasure finished design size:
14-count paper– 3³⁄₈ x 2³⁄₄ inches

DECK THE BOUGHS

Instructions

Zigzag-stitch or overcast the edges of the large piece of Aida cloth to prevent fraying. Find the center of the chart and the center of the Aida cloth; begin stitching there. Use two plies of floss to work the cross-stitches. Work all the backstitches using one ply of the floss.

Centering the design, trim the stitched Aida rectangle to measure 4×3¼". Pin the Aida pieces with wrong sides together and raw edges even. Use one strand of the metallic gold thread to work running stitches through both layers of the fabric ⅜" from the edges, leaving the top edge open.

Lightly stuff the ornament with polyester fiberfill. Work running stitches across the top of the ornament. For the hanger, thread a needle with a 6" length of the metallic gold thread. Tack the ends of the thread to the top corners of the ornament.

Stars Elf

ELF ORNAMENTS

Anchor		DMC	
387	·		Ecru
893	♥	224	Shell pink
1014	✕	355	Terra cotta
878	#	501	Dark blue green
875	☐	503	True blue green
890	★	729	Old gold
378	◇	841	Beige brown
381	●	938	Coffee brown
1010	❘	951	Ivory
887	⊘	3046	Medium yellow beige
886	⟋	3047	Light yellow beige

BACKSTITCH

381	⟋	938	Coffee brown – all backstitches (1X)

Candy Cane Elf stitch count: 52 high x 38 wide
Candy Cane Elf finished design sizes:
18-count fabric – 2⅞ x 2⅛ inches
14-count fabric – 3¾ x 2¾ inches
11-count fabric – 4¾ x 3½ inches
Painter Elf stitch count: 53 high x 40 wide
Painter Elf finished design sizes:
18-count fabric – 3 x 2¼ inches
14-count fabric – 3¾ x 2⅞ inches
11-count fabric – 4⅞ x 3⅝ inches
Stars Elf stitch count: 52 high x 33 wide
Stars Elf finished design sizes:
18-count fabric – 2⅞ x 1⅞ inches
14-count fabric – 3¾ x 2⅜ inches
11-count fabric – 4¾ x 3 inches

Painter Elf

Candy Cane Elf

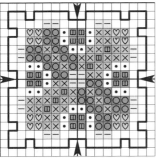

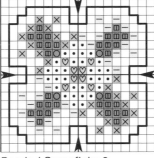

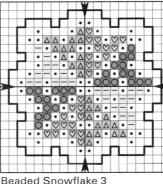

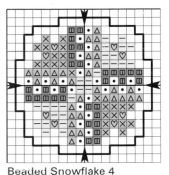

Beaded Snowflake 1
Finished design size:
14-count plastic—1 x 1 inch

Beaded Snowflake 2
Finished design size:
14-count plastic—1 x 1 inch

Beaded Snowflake 3
Finished design size:
14-count plastic—1⅛ x 1⅛ inch

Beaded Snowflake 4
Finished design size:
14-count plastic—1 x 1 inch

BEADED SNOWFLAKE ORNAMENTS

As shown on page 68.

Fabric and Floss
For each ornament
3×3" piece of 14-count silver
perforated paper
White embroidery floss

Supplies
Needle
Seed beads in colors listed in the
key, *far right*
Kreinik 002 silver #8 braid

Instructions
Begin stitching near one corner of the paper. Carefully count holes to be sure there is enough room to complete the design. To secure the first bead, cut and separate a single ply of floss, 36" in length. Fold the floss in half and thread both cut ends through the needle. Bring the needle through the first hole in the paper from the back. Slip the bead on the needle, insert the needle through the second hole, and then through the loop formed by folding the thread; pull firmly.

Continue adding beads, using half cross-stitches. Work in complete rows, changing bead colors as you come to them. To end a thread, run the tail under stitches on the back or through a long row of beads. Trim the finished stitchery one square beyond the beaded area. For the hanger, attach a 5" length of silver braid to the top of the design.

PIPECLEANER ELVES

As shown on page 69, finished elves are 4½ to 4¾" tall.

Fabric and Thread
For each elf
6×8½" piece of 14-count white
perforated paper
Cotton embroidery floss in colors
listed in the key on *page 76*
Kreinik metallic threads in colors
and sizes listed in the key on
page 76

Supplies
Needle
Two 2"-long red or green chenille
stems
Two 1½"-long white chenille stems
Crafts glue
Two ⅜"-diameter gold jingle bells
Monofilament

Instructions
Begin stitching near one corner of the perforated paper. Carefully count the holes to be sure there is enough room to complete each section of each elf. Use three plies of floss or one strand of metallic thread to work the cross stitches. Work the French knots using two plies of floss. Work the blended-needle stitches as specified in the key on *page 76*. Work the backstitches using two plies of floss or one strand of the metallic thread.

Trim the finished stitchery one square beyond the stitched area. Use the stitched pieces as patterns to cut matching backs from the remaining perforated paper.

Trim the chenille away from a ¼"-long area at each end of the chenille

BEADED SNOWFLAKE ORNAMENTS
Mill Hill Beads

•	00161	Crystal Seed Bead
⊙	0020	Sapphire Seed Bead
⊞	00252	Iris Seed Bead
△	02006	Ice Blue Seed Bead
✕	02008	Sea Breeze Seed Bead
—	02017	Crystal Aqua Seed Bead
♡	02024	Heather Mauve Seed Bead

stems. Glue the exposed wire of the chenille stem to the wrong side of the stitched body at the arm and leg positions. Glue the stitched feet and hands to the opposite ends of the chenille stems. With the edges of the paper even, glue the matching perforated paper backs to each shape.

Sew a jingle bell to each of the elf's shoes. Bend the arms and legs as desired. Thead an 8" length of monofilament through the top of the ornament for a hanger; knot the ends of the monofilament together.

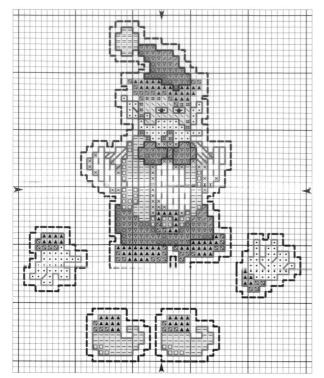

Boss Elf

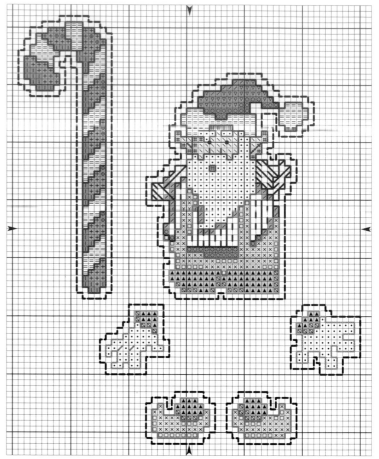

Candy Cane Elf

Boss Elf stitch count: 57 high x 46 wide
Boss Elf finished design sizes:
14-count paper – 4 1/8 x 3 1/4 inches
10-count paper – 5 3/4 x 4 5/8 inches
7-count paper – 8 1/4 x 6 1/2 inches

Candy Cane Elf stitch count: 72 high x 57 wide
Candy Cane Elf finished design sizes:
14-count paper – 5 1/4 x 4 1/8 inches
10-count paper – 7 1/4 x 5 3/4 inches
7-count paper – 10 1/4 x 8 1/4 inches

Worker Elf stitch count: 48 high x 44 wide
Worker Elf finished design sizes:
14-count paper – 3 1/2 x 3 1/4 inches
10-count paper – 4 7/8 x 4 1/2 inches
7-count paper – 6 7/8 x 6 1/4 inches

Worker Elf

PIPECLEANER ELVES

Anchor		DMC	
002	·	000	White
334	▽	606	True Orange red
332	◢	608	True Orange
046	◉	666	Red
228	▢	700	Medium Christmas green
226	▭	702	Light Christmas green
238	☒	703	Chartreuse
944	⊙	869	Hazel
381	◆	938	Coffee brown
4146	#	950	Light rose beige
778	◺	3774	Pale rose beige
	✳	001	Kreinik silver #8 braid
	◉	011C	Kreinik nickel #8 braid
	◩	1700	Kreinik misty gold Ombre
	▲	2000	Kreinik solid gold Ombre
	▤	3200	Kreinik solid pearl Ombre

Anchor		DMC	
BLENDED NEEDLE			
334	⊞	606	True Orange red (2X) and 003 Kreinik red blending filament (1X)
332	⊕	608	True Orange (2X) and 003 Kreinik red blending filament (1X)
046	⊡	666	Red (2X) and 003 Kreinik red blending filament (1X)
BACKSTITCH			
002	╱	000	White – hair, beard and eyebrows
400	╱	317	Pewter – mittens
046	╱	666	Red – shirt, hats, pants, tie, and gloves
228	╱	700	Medium Christmas green – overalls, shoes, shirt, and vest

Anchor		DMC	
381	╱	938	Coffee brown – hammer handle, hair, mouth and nose of Worker Elf
883	╱	3064	Cocoa – faces
	╱	011C	Kreinik nickel #8 braid – tool box and hammer
	╱	1700	Kreinik misty gold Ombre – shoes, apron of Worker Elf, gloves and clothing of Candy Cane Elf
	╱	2000	Kreinik solid gold Ombre – gloves, buckle, and clothing of Boss Elf
	╱	3200	Kreinik solid pearl Ombre – candy cane, fur
FRENCH KNOT			
381	●	938	Coffee brown – eyes

NUTCRACKER ORNAMENT

As shown on page 70, the finished nutcracker is 6½"-tall.

Fabric and Thread

Two 12×8" pieces of 28-count antique white Monaco fabric
Cotton embroidery floss in colors listed in the key
Metallic threads as listed in the key
⅛ yard of lightweight fusible interfacing

Supplies

Needle; embroidery hoop
Seed beads in colors listed in the key
Air-soluble fabric marker
7" length of ⅛"-diameter gold cord
Polyester fiberfill
½ yard of ¼"-diameter blue-and-gold cord
Crafts glue

Instructions

Zigzag-stitch or overcast the edges of the fabric to prevent fraying. Find the center of one piece of Monaco fabric and the center of the nutcracker chart; begin stitching there.

Use three plies of floss or one strand of braid to work the cross-stitches over two threads of fabric. Work the backstitches using one ply of floss. Use two plies of matching floss to attach the beads. Place the stitchery facedown on a soft towel and carefully press from the back.

Fuse the interfacing to the back of the stitched piece following the manufacturer's instructions. Use the air-soluble marker to draw the ornament oval onto the fabric as indicated on the chart; cut out. Center the pattern over the stitched piece; cut out. Cut the back fabric oval in the same manner.

For the hanger, fold the gold cord in half to make a loop. With raw edges of the cord even with raw edges of top center back, sew the hanger to the right side of the back. With right sides together, pin the front to the back, being careful that the cord is on the inside. Sew, using a ¼" seam, leaving an opening at the side for turning. Turn the ornament right side out, press lightly, and fill with polyester fiberfill. Hand-sew the opening closed.

Hand-sew the blue-and-gold cord around outside edge of the ornament over the seam. Use crafts glue on the ends of the trim to prevent fraying.

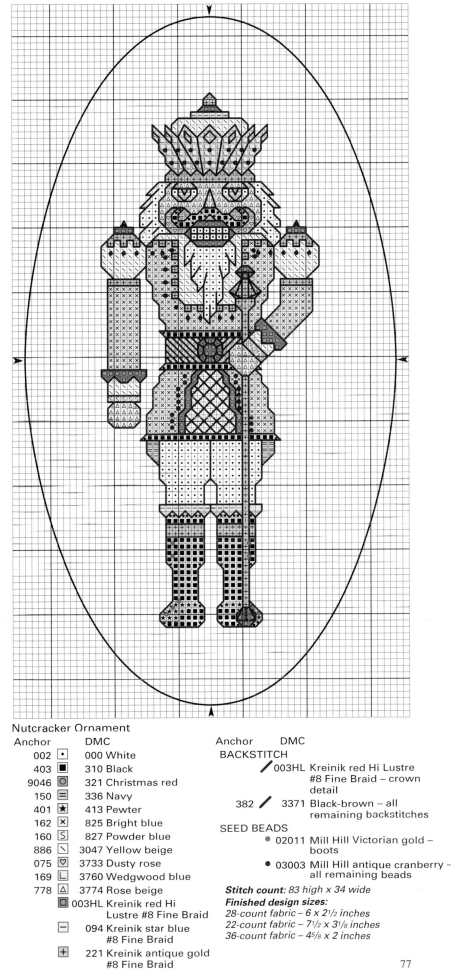

Nutcracker Ornament

Anchor		DMC	
002	·	000	White
403	■	310	Black
9046	◐	321	Christmas red
150	⊟	336	Navy
401	★	413	Pewter
162	✕	825	Bright blue
160	S	827	Powder blue
886	◪	3047	Yellow beige
075	♡	3733	Dusty rose
169	L	3760	Wedgwood blue
778	△	3774	Rose beige
	▨	003HL	Kreinik red Hi Lustre #8 Fine Braid
	⊟	094	Kreinik star blue #8 Fine Braid
	➕	221	Kreinik antique gold #8 Fine Braid

Anchor		DMC	
BACKSTITCH			
	╱	003HL	Kreinik red Hi Lustre #8 Fine Braid – crown detail
382	╱	3371	Black-brown – all remaining backstitches
SEED BEADS			
	●	02011	Mill Hill Victorian gold – boots
	●	03003	Mill Hill antique cranberry – all remaining beads

Stitch count: 83 high x 34 wide
Finished design sizes:
28-count fabric – 6 x 2½ inches
22-count fabric – 7½ x 3⅛ inches
36-count fabric – 4⅝ x 2 inches

DECK THE BOUGHS

SNOWFLAKE MEDALLION ORNAMENTS

As shown on pages 70 and 71, the finished ornaments are 3¼x3¼".

Fabric and Thread

For each ornament
8×8" piece of 30-count white Murano fabric
4¾×4¾" piece of lightweight fusible interfacing
3⅝×3⅝" piece of white felt
Cotton embroidery floss in colors listed in the key
Kreinik metallic thread as listed in the key

For each tassel
One skein of pale old gold (DMC 677) floss
1 spool each of Kreinik 003 red and 002 gold #8 braid
1 spool of Kreinik 008 green blending filament
1 spool of Kreinik 2000 gold Ombre thread

Supplies
Needle; embroidery hoop
3⅝×3⅝" piece of self-stick mounting board with foam
18" length of ¼"-wide metallic gold flat braided trim
18" length of ⅛"-diameter red-and-gold cord
7" length of gold cord
Crafts glue
3×3-inch piece of cardboard

Instructions
Zigzag-stitch or overcast the edges of each piece of the fabric to prevent fraying. Find the center of one piece of the fabric and the center of the desired chart; begin stitching there. Use one strand of the braid to work the cross-stitches over two threads of the fabric. Work the backstitches using one strand of the braid.

Use one ply of floss to work backstitch guidelines to mark the placement of the curved couching and buttonhole stitches. Work the backstitches, buttonhole stitches, lazy daisy stitches, ribbed spider web stitches, stem stitches, and the

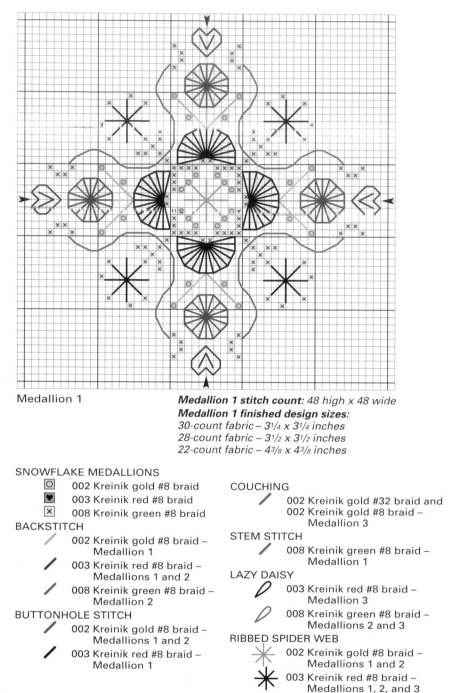

Medallion 1

Medallion 1 stitch count: *48 high x 48 wide*
Medallion 1 finished design sizes:
30-count fabric – 3¼ x 3¼ inches
28-count fabric – 3½ x 3½ inches
22-count fabric – 4⅜ x 4⅜ inches

SNOWFLAKE MEDALLIONS
- ◎ 002 Kreinik gold #8 braid
- ♥ 003 Kreinik red #8 braid
- ✕ 008 Kreinik green #8 braid

BACKSTITCH
- 002 Kreinik gold #8 braid – Medallion 1
- 003 Kreinik red #8 braid – Medallions 1 and 2
- 008 Kreinik green #8 braid – Medallion 2

BUTTONHOLE STITCH
- 002 Kreinik gold #8 braid – Medallions 1 and 2
- 003 Kreinik red #8 braid – Medallion 1

COUCHING
- 002 Kreinik gold #32 braid and 002 Kreinik gold #8 braid – Medallion 3

STEM STITCH
- 008 Kreinik green #8 braid – Medallion 1

LAZY DAISY
- 003 Kreinik red #8 braid – Medallion 3
- 008 Kreinik green #8 braid – Medallions 2 and 3

RIBBED SPIDER WEB
- ✳ 002 Kreinik gold #8 braid – Medallions 1 and 2
- ✳ 003 Kreinik red #8 braid – Medallions 1, 2, and 3

couching stitches as specified in the key and referring to the diagrams, *opposite.* Place the finished stitchery facedown on a soft towel and press from the back.

Fuse the interfacing to the back of the stitchery following the manufacturer's instructions. Peel the protective paper from the mounting board. Center and position the back of the fabric on the foam side of the mounting board; press to stick. Trim the fabric ½" beyond the mounting

board. Fold the excess fabric to back; glue. Position and glue the gold trim around the front of the ornament, leaving the first and last ½" free. Position and glue the red and gold cord inside the gold braid, gluing the raw ends to the back. Finish gluing gold braid, gluing raw ends to back.

For the tassel, cut a 6" strand of the floss and an 18-inch strand of the Ombre thread; set aside. Wrap 4 single strands of floss, 1 strand *each* of

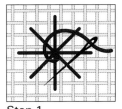

Couching Stitch

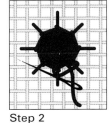

Step 1

Step 2

Ribbed Spider Web Stitch

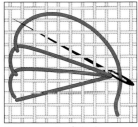

Buttonhole Stitch

Lazy Daisy

Stem Stitch

green and red #8 braid, and 3 strands of gold #8 braid around cardboard 11 times. Thread the 6" strand under the threads at one end of the cardboard; tie. For the hanger, fold the gold cord in half; glue the ends to top center of the ornament back. Cut the thread at the opposite edge of the cardboard; remove. Wrap the 18" strand around the bundle ³⁄₈" below the tied end. Trim the tassel ends; glue to back of the ornament. Glue the felt to the back of the ornament.

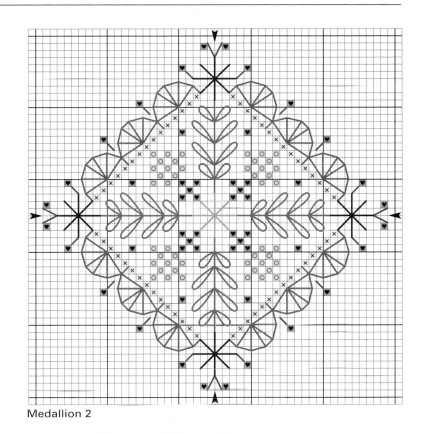

Medallion 2

Medallion 2 stitch count: 48 high x 48 wide
Medallion 2 finished design sizes:
30-count fabric – 3¹⁄₄ x 3¹⁄₄ inches
28-count fabric – 3¹⁄₂ x 3¹⁄₂ inches
22-count fabric – 4³⁄₈ x 4³⁄₈ inches

Medallion 3 stitch count: 47 high x 47 wide
Medallion 3 finished design sizes:
30-count fabric – 3¹⁄₈ x 3¹⁄₈ inches
28-count fabric – 3³⁄₈ x 3³⁄₈ inches
22-count fabric – 4¹⁄₄ x 4¹⁄₄ inches

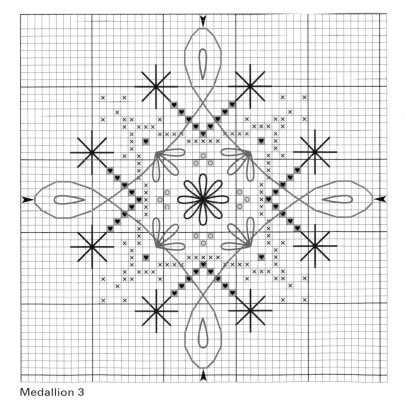

Medallion 3

Adam
Amy
Amanda
Annie
Andy
Ben
Barbie
Blair
Bobby
Clare
Charlie

Santa's MAGIC

Santa Claus, Saint Nicholas, Kriss Kringle—regardless of the name we give him or the cut of his cap and cloak, he's always in style come Christmastime. Our collection of six charming Santas that you can display or wear is a delight to stitch for Christmas decorating and gift giving.

Surrounded by a flourish of colorful holly with bright-red berries, our gentle Saint Nicholas wears his usual array of traditional red-and-white splendor. While preparing for his midnight ride, he enjoys the Christmas Eve indulgence of a tug or two on his pipe. The sack of gaily wrapped gifts is a preview of what's in store for children of all ages! Designer Ruth Schmuff of Randallstown, Maryland, used 28-count white Brittney fabric and embellished the edges of Santa's cap and sleeves with white furlike turkey-work stitches sprinkled with pearly glitter.

An arch of golden Smyrna cross-stitches accents the traditional portrait beautifully. Spectacularly framed, the piece surely will become a cherished family heirloom.

SANTA'S MAGIC

Up, up, and away! When Dancer and Prancer are too tired to go any further, Santa has other means for travel at his disposal. The gifts need guaranteed overnight delivery, and Santa will get them to their destination by hook or by crook—or even by balloon! Designer Mike Vickery of White, Georgia, used Aida cloth and made sure all those glasses of milk and platters of cookies wouldn't have any ill effect on Santa's airborne mobility.

Whimsically dimensional, these beaded perforated-plastic figures show Santa Claus in true form—going down the chimney carrying gifts.

The charming duo measures 4 and 5 inches tall and fastens to a garment with pin backs. Teresa G. Hanson of Wautauga, Texas, designed the components on flat pieces of plastic canvas that you assemble with glue.

SANTA'S MAGIC

Decorating our homes for the holidays is a much-anticipated ritual that challenges our creativity and practicality at the same time. Designer Helen Nicholson of Woodstock, Georgia, fashioned a circle of Santas to dress up a fabulous poinsettia. It would look equally bright encircling a tiny tabletop Christmas tree. A few colors of floss and a sheet of perforated paper are all you need to create this perky pot decoration—quick-and-easy home decorating at its very best.

Top your tree with a festive flourish; here's one that's destined to become a family favorite. His arms laden with toys, our dot-and-plaid Saint Nicholas tree topper stands tall with the help of a plastic-canvas stabilizing insert. Worked on moss green Jobelan fabric, he'll offer hours of stitching enjoyment. Lois Winston of Elkins Park, Pennsylvania, designed the three-dimensional figure so you can stuff and finish it as a collectible stand-up Santa.

Santa's Magic

ST. NICK

As shown on page 80.

Fabric and Thread

14×16" piece of 28-count white Brittney fabric

Cotton embroidery floss in colors listed in the key

Three additional skeins of white floss

Kreinik #4 braid in colors listed in the key

Kreinik blending filament in colors listed in the key

One additional spool of Kreinik 032 pearl filament

Supplies

Needle
Embroidery hoop
Desired frame and mat

Instructions

Zigzag-stitch or overcast the edges of the fabric to prevent fraying. Find the center of the chart and the center of the fabric; begin stitching there. Use three plies of floss or one strand of braid to work the cross-stitches over two threads of the fabric. Work the backstitches using one ply of floss or one strand of cord.

Referring to the Turkey Work diagrams, *right*, use three plies of floss and one strand of filament to make the turkey-work stitches on the sleeve cuffs and the hat trim.

Work the Smyrna cross-stitches using one strand of braid and referring to the diagram, *below*. Press the finished stitchery from the back. Mat and frame the piece as desired.

Smyrna
Cross Stitch

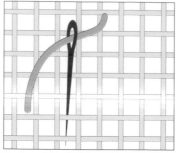

Turkey Work Step 1

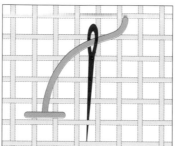

Turkey Work Step 2

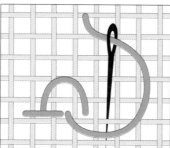

Turkey Work Step 3

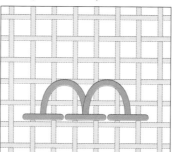

Turkey Work Step 4

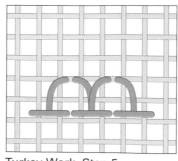

Turkey Work Step 5

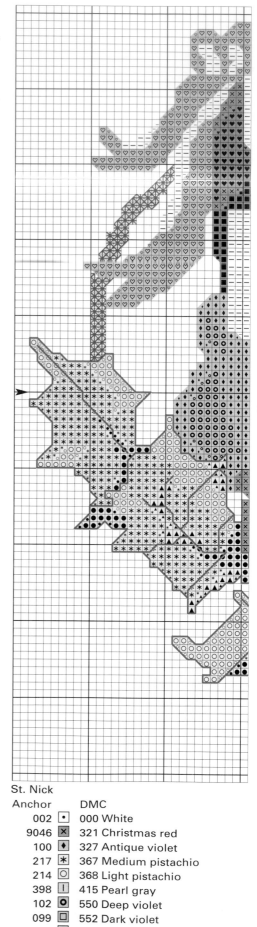

St. Nick

Anchor		DMC	
002	·	000	White
9046	✕	321	Christmas red
100	◆	327	Antique violet
217	✳	367	Medium pistachio
214	○	368	Light pistachio
398	I	415	Pearl gray
102	◉	550	Deep violet
099	▢	552	Dark violet
1012	✴	754	Peach

Anchor		DMC
1021	⁄	761 Light salmon
136	☆	799 Delft blue
043	♥	815 Medium garnet
218	▲	890 Deep pistachio
897	■	902 Deep garnet
246	●	986 Forest green
1023	▽	3712 Medium salmon
273	#	3787 Brown gray
	◇	009 Kreinik emerald #4 very fine braid
	▨	102 Kreinik copper #4 very fine braid

Anchor		DMC
	—	221 Kreinik white #4 very fine braid

TURKEY WORK

002	⊞	000 White and 032 Kreinik pearl blending filament (1X)

BACKSTITCH

379	╱	840 Beige brown – face
	╱	009 Kreinik emerald blending filament – leaves (1X)
	╱	105C Kreinik antique silver cord – smoke (1X)

Anchor		DMC

SMYRNA CROSS-STITCH

	✳	002 Kreinik gold #4 very fine braid (1X) – border

Stitch count: *98 high x 117 wide*
Finished design sizes:
28-count fabric – 7 x 8³/₈ inches
22-count fabric – 9 x 10⁵/₈ inches
36-count fabric – 5¹/₂ x 6¹/₂ inches

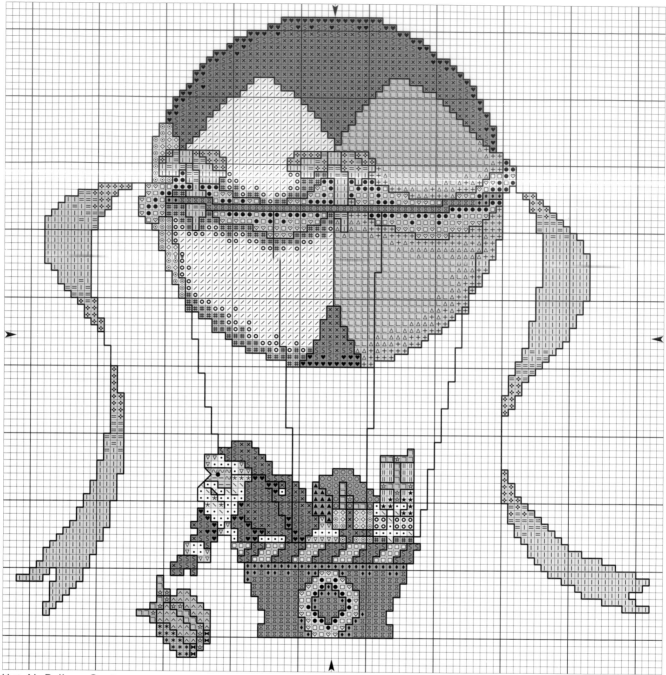

Hot-Air Balloon Santa

Anchor		DMC
002	▫	000 White (3X)
038	❖	335 Medium rose
008	∼	353 Dark peach
310	◆	434 Chestnut
1045	▨	436 Tan
099	⋈	552 Dark violet
098	✳	553 Medium violet
096	∧	554 Light violet
830	★	644 Light beige gray
046	S	666 Red
886	⊡	677 Pale old gold
228	●	700 Medium Christmas green
226	▢	702 Light Christmas green
256	▽	704 Chartreuse

Anchor		DMC
088	▲	718 Plum
305	⊙	725 True topaz
293	╱	727 Pale topaz
890	☆	729 Medium old gold
234	▽	762 Pearl gray
307	▦	783 Christmas gold
131	⊙	798 Dark Delft blue
130	◇	809 True Delft blue
1005	♥	816 Garnet
023	∥	818 Pink
390	╲	822 Pale beige gray
257	★	905 Dark parrot green
255	‖	907 Light parrot green
1011	▬	948 Light peach
187	✚	958 True aqua

Anchor		DMC
186	△	959 Medium aqua
185	L	964 Light aqua
036	▤	3326 Pale rose
086	◎	3608 Fuchsia
035	✖	3705 Watermelon

BACKSTITCH
403 ╱ 310 Black – all backstitches

FRENCH KNOT
403 ● 310 Black – Santa's eye

Stitch count: 95 high x 94 wide
Finished design sizes:
14-count fabric – 6¾ x 6¾ inches
11-count fabric – 8⅝ x 8½ inches
18-count fabric – 5¼ x 5¼ inches

HOT-AIR BALLOON SANTA

As shown on page 82.

Fabric and Floss
15×15" piece of 14-count white
  Aida cloth
Cotton embroidery floss in colors
  listed in key

Supplies
Needle
Embroidery hoop
Desired frame and mat

Instructions
Zigzag-stitch or overcast the edges
of the Adia cloth to prevent fraying.
Find the center of the chart and the
center of the fabric; begin stitching
there. Use three plies of floss to
work the cross-stitches. Work the
French knot using two plies of floss.
Work the backstitches using one ply
of floss. Press the finished stitchery
from the back. Mat and frame the
piece as desired.

SANTA PINS

*As shown on page 83, Santa pins
are 3" tall.*

Fabric and Thread
For the Santa Ringer
4×6" piece of 14-count clear
  perforated plastic
Cotton embroidery floss in colors
  listed in the key
Wildflowers Passion cotton thread
4×3" piece of red felt
For the Down the Chimney Santa
4×6" piece of 14-count clear
  perforated plastic
Cotton embroidery floss in colors
  listed in the key *on page 90*
4×3" piece of red felt

Supplies
Needle
Seed beads in colors listed in the
  key *right and on page 90*
Scissors
Crafts glue
1"-long pin back
All-purpose adhesive

Continued

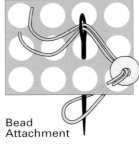

Bead
Attachment

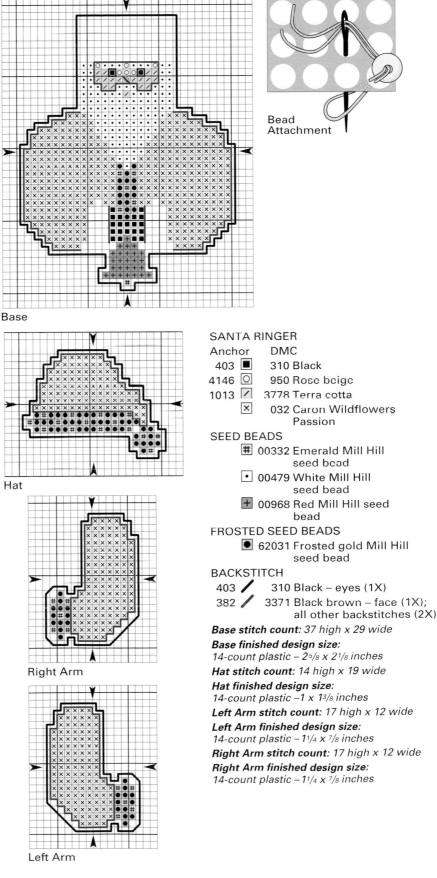

Base

Hat

Right Arm

Left Arm

SANTA RINGER

Anchor		DMC	
403	■	310	Black
4146	○	950	Rose beige
1013	╱	3778	Terra cotta
	☒	032	Caron Wildflowers Passion

SEED BEADS
	⌗	00332	Emerald Mill Hill seed bead
	•	00479	White Mill Hill seed bead
	⊞	00968	Red Mill Hill seed bead

FROSTED SEED BEADS
	●	62031	Frosted gold Mill Hill seed bead

BACKSTITCH
403	╱	310	Black – eyes (1X)
382	╱	3371	Black brown – face (1X); all other backstitches (2X)

Base stitch count: 37 high x 29 wide
Base finished design size:
14-count plastic – 2⁵⁄₈ x 2¹⁄₈ inches
Hat stitch count: 14 high x 19 wide
Hat finished design size:
14-count plastic –1 x 1³⁄₈ inches
Left Arm stitch count: 17 high x 12 wide
Left Arm finished design size:
14-count plastic –1¹⁄₄ x ⁷⁄₈ inches
Right Arm stitch count: 17 high x 12 wide
Right Arm finished design size:
14-count plastic –1¹⁄₄ x ⁷⁄₈ inches

SANTA'S MAGIC

Continued from page 89

Instructions

Begin stitching near one corner of the perforated plastic. Carefully count the holes to be sure there is enough room on the perforated plastic to complete all sections of the Santa design.

For the Ringer Santa Pin, use two plies of floss to work the cross-stitches. Work the backstitches using one ply of floss. For Santa's coat, hat, and sleeves, use one strand of the Wildflowers thread to work the cross-stitches, completing each cross-stitch before beginning the next stitch.

For both pins, to secure the first bead, cut and separate a single ply of 36"-long floss. Fold the floss in half and thread both cut ends through the needle. From the front, bring the needle up through the first hole in the plastic. Slip the bead on the needle. Insert the needle through the second hole, then through the loop formed by folding the thread in half, and pull firmly (*see the diagram on page 89*).

Continue adding beads to the plastic using half cross-stitches and working in complete rows. To end a thread, run the tail under the stitches on the back or through the center of a long row of beads.

Trim the stitched pieces to one square beyond the beaded and stitched areas. Use the Santa body as a pattern to cut a matching back from the felt. Referring to the photograph, *page 83*, position and glue the pieces together. Glue the felt to the back of the pin. Attach the pin back using the all-purpose cement.

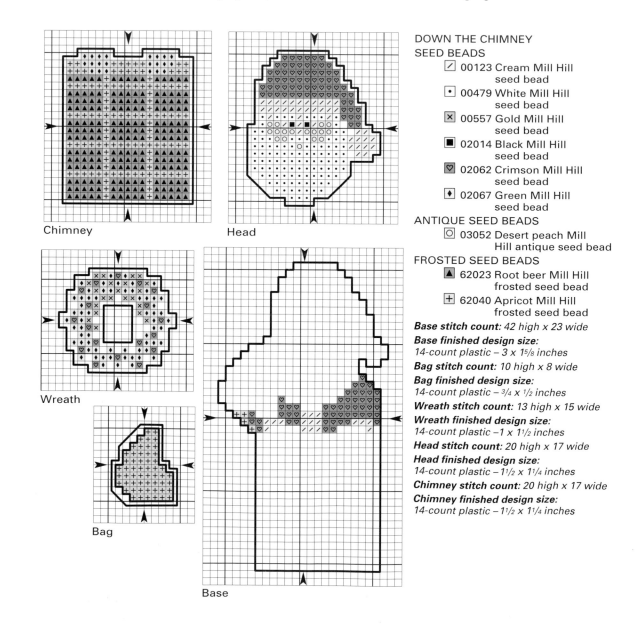

Chimney

Head

Wreath

Bag

Base

DOWN THE CHIMNEY
SEED BEADS
- ☑ 00123 Cream Mill Hill seed bead
- • 00479 White Mill Hill seed bead
- ☒ 00557 Gold Mill Hill seed bead
- ■ 02014 Black Mill Hill seed bead
- ♡ 02062 Crimson Mill Hill seed bead
- ◆ 02067 Green Mill Hill seed bead

ANTIQUE SEED BEADS
- ◯ 03052 Desert peach Mill Hill antique seed bead

FROSTED SEED BEADS
- ▲ 62023 Root beer Mill Hill frosted seed bead
- ⊞ 62040 Apricot Mill Hill frosted seed bead

Base stitch count: 42 high x 23 wide
Base finished design size:
14-count plastic – 3 x 1⅝ inches
Bag stitch count: 10 high x 8 wide
Bag finished design size:
14-count plastic – ¾ x ½ inches
Wreath stitch count: 13 high x 15 wide
Wreath finished design size:
14-count plastic –1 x 1½ inches
Head stitch count: 20 high x 17 wide
Head finished design size:
14-count plastic – 1½ x 1¼ inches
Chimney stitch count: 20 high x 17 wide
Chimney finished design size:
14-count plastic – 1½ x 1¼ inches

SANTA GARLAND

As shown on page 84.

Fabric and Floss

For four Santa motifs:
3×11" piece of 14-count white
    perforated paper
Cotton embroidery floss in
    colors listed in the key

Supplies

Needle

Instructions

Find the center between two
Santas on the chart and the
center of the perforated paper;
begin stitching there. Use two
plies of the floss to work the
cross-stitches.

Work the backstitches with
one ply of floss. Make the
French knots using two plies of
floss. Trim the finished stitchery one square beyond the
stitched area.

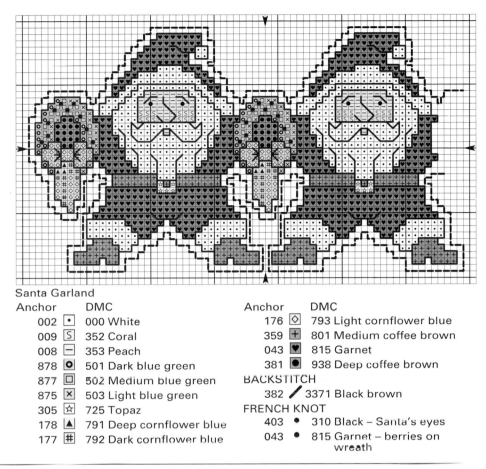

Santa Garland

Anchor		DMC		Anchor		DMC
002	•	000 White		176	◇	793 Light cornflower blue
009	S	352 Coral		359	+	801 Medium coffee brown
008	−	353 Peach		043	♥	815 Garnet
878	◉	501 Dark blue green		381	●	938 Deep coffee brown
877	□	502 Medium blue green		**BACKSTITCH**		
875	✕	503 Light blue green		382	╱	3371 Black brown
305	☆	725 Topaz		**FRENCH KNOT**		
178	▲	791 Deep cornflower blue		403	•	310 Black – Santa's eyes
177	#	792 Dark cornflower blue		043	•	815 Garnet – berries on wreath

SANTA TREE TOPPER

*As shown on page 85, finished
Santa is 11¼" tall.*

Fabric and Thread

17×13" piece of 28-count moss
    green Jobelan fabric
12×8-inch piece of polyester fleece
12×8-inch-piece of burgundy-print
    cotton fabric
12×8-inch piece of lightweight
    iron-on interfacing
Cotton embroidery floss in colors
    listed in the key on *page 92*
Kreinik #8 braid in color listed in
    the key on *page 92*

Supplies

Needle
Embroidery hoop
Crafts glue
Fine-line permanent marker

Matching sewing thread
1¼ yards of ¼"-diameter gold-
    and-burgundy cord
9×12-inch piece of 14-count clear
    plastic canvas for stabilizer

Instructions

Zigzag-stitch or overcast the edges
of the Jobelan fabric to prevent fraying. Find the center of the chart and
the center of the fabric; begin stitching there. Use three plies of floss or
one strand of the braid to work the
cross-stitches over two threads of the
fabric. Work the French knots using
one ply of floss. Work the backstitches using one ply of floss.

Press the finished stitchery from
the back. Baste the fleece to the
wrong side of the Jobelan fabric, ¼"
beyond the stitching. Following the
manufacturer's instructions, fuse the
interfacing to the wrong side of the
burgundy-print fabric. With right
sides together, sew the front to the

back along the basting line, leaving
the bottom open. Trim the seam
allowances to ¼".

Trim the bottom front edge of the
stitched fabric ¾" beyond the cross-
stitches, and the bottom back edge
even with the front. For the hem,
turn up the bottom edge ½" and
press; hand-sew in place. Clip the
curves, turn, and press.

Carefully trace the tree topper's
shape onto the plastic canvas with
the marker. Cut out about ⅛" inside
the traced line. Insert the plastic canvas shape into the fabric Santa. Glue
or hand-sew the cord over the seam
line and along the entire bottom edge
of the tree topper. *Note: When placing the topper on the tree, make sure
that the plastic canvas is between the
stitched front and the tree top.*

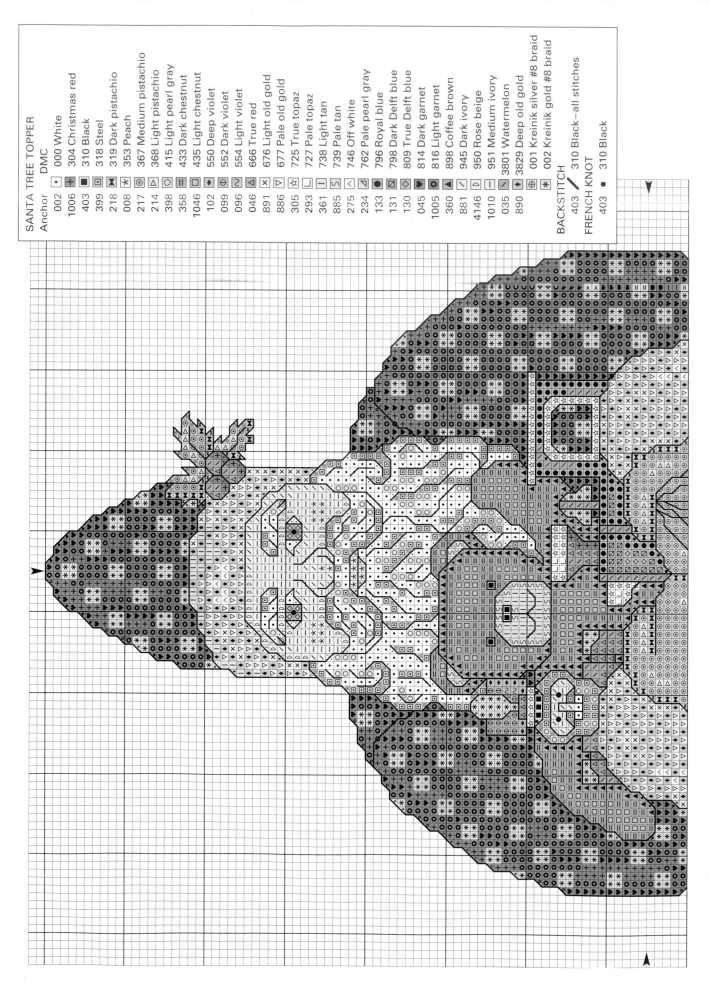

SANTA TREE TOPPER

Anchor	DMC	
002	•	000 White
1006	+	304 Christmas red
403	■	310 Black
399	⊡	318 Steel
218	✕	319 Dark pistachio
008	✳	353 Peach
217	⊙	367 Medium pistachio
214	△	368 Light pistachio
398	⊘	415 Light pearl gray
358	‖	433 Dark chestnut
1046	▢	435 Light chestnut
102	◆	550 Deep violet
099	⊕	552 Dark violet
096	⊃	554 Light violet
046	◁	666 True red
891	✕	676 Light old gold
886	▷	677 Pale old gold
305	☆	725 True topaz
293	⌐	727 Pale topaz
361	⏐	738 Light tan
885	S	739 Pale tan
275	∢	746 Off white
234	◿	762 Pale pearl gray
133	●	796 Royal blue
131	⊘	798 Dark Delft blue
130	◇	809 True Delft blue
045	◣	814 Dark garnet
1005	◙	816 Light garnet
360	◀	898 Coffee brown
881	⁄	945 Dark ivory
4146	◹	950 Rose beige
1010	⎮	951 Medium ivory
035	╱	3801 Watermelon
890	◆	3829 Deep old gold
001	⊕	Kreinik silver #8 braid
002	✳	Kreinik gold #8 braid

BACKSTITCH
403 ╱ 310 Black—all stitches

FRENCH KNOT
403 • 310 Black

SANTA'S MAGIC

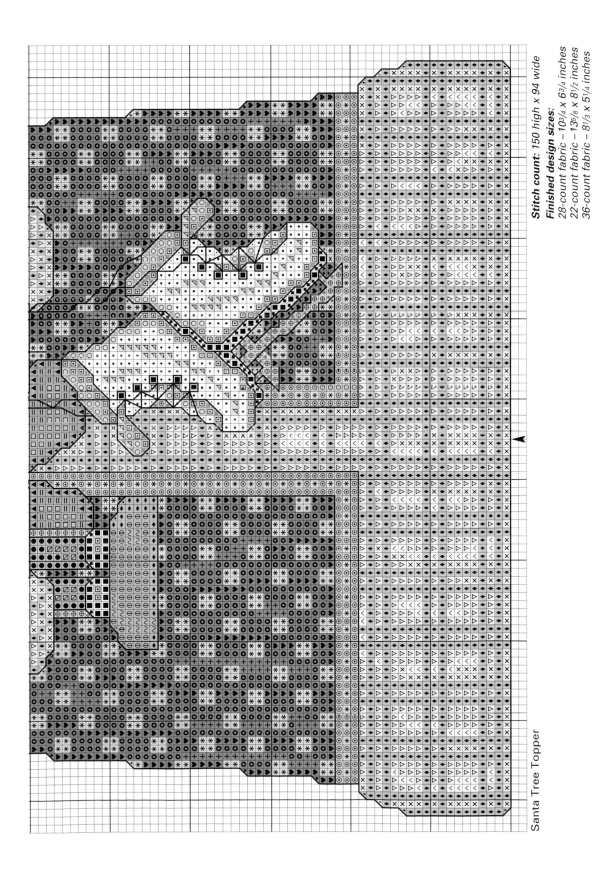

Stitch count: 150 high x 94 wide
Finished design sizes:
28-count fabric – 10³/₄ x 6³/₄ inches
22-count fabric – 13⁵/₈ x 8¹/₂ inches
36-count fabric – 8¹/₃ x 5¹/₄ inches

Santa Tree Topper

Symbols OF THE SEASON

Make your loved ones' holiday homecoming picture-perfect with this remarkable collection of cross-stitched designs. The elegant table set shown here— as well as the festive towel and napkin, merry kitchen accessories, and sparkling Hardanger sampler on the following pages—are welcome additions to any home.

Angels, forever heralded as the messengers of Christ's birth, are beautifully interpreted in this table runner and coordinating napkin set. Stitched over two threads on 25-count mushroom Lugana fabric, these shimmering angelic table linens will set an elegant tone at all of your holiday festivities.

Designer Barbara Sestok of Germantown, New York, has produced an exquisite design that captures the majestic splendor of the season. Metallic threads and shimmering seed beads provide sparkling accents. The pieces are trimmed with glittering red braid and a frame of scalloped metallic-gold lace for the perfect finishing touches.

Designer Barbara Sestok of Germantown, New York, chose two classic Yuletide symbols for the merry kitchen accessories shown on these pages. They're as pretty as they are functional, and any host or hostess would appreciate receiving them.

Poinsettias and hearts combine to make the elegant towel and napkin ensemble. The repeat motif is stitched across the Aida-cloth insert on a purchased towel. A single poinsettia motif adorns the prefinished napkin.

The napkin and pot holder shown *above,* also designed by Barbara Sestok, are guaranteed to spread holiday warmth wherever friends and family gather.

The pot holder has a handy opening for ease of stitching on the Aida-fabric insert. The prefinished napkin displays a simplified version of the bell motif so it won't take forever to stitch up a set of four or six napkins.

SYMBOLS OF THE SEASON

Bring the warmth of the holidays into your home by filling it with your own works of art. The project, *above,* will show off your stitching skills.

Hardanger designer Rosalyn Watnemo of Fargo, North Dakota, used exquisite stitches and sparkling metallic gold thread on 25-count gold-and-cream Lugana fabric to create this striking sampler destined to become a treasured heirloom.

This elegant Christmas sampler is a classic combination of Hardanger stitches and the delicate open areas of the design worked in metallic threads.

The heartfelt sentiment "All Hearts Come Home for Christmas," expressed in stitches, reminds us of the things we value most at this special time of the year—home and family.

NAPKIN

As shown on page 94, the finished napkin measures 14½×14½".

Fabric and Thread

For each napkin

15×15" piece of 25-count mushroom Lugana fabric

Cotton embroidery floss in colors listed in the key

Kreinik #8 braid in colors listed in the key

Supplies

Needle; embroidery hoop

1⅔ yards of ¾"-wide metallic gold flat lace

Matching sewing thread

Instructions

Zigzag-stitch or overcast the edges of the fabric to prevent fraying. Measure 2⅛" from the left edge and 1⅜" from the bottom; begin stitching the bottom left stitch of the instrument chart there. Use three plies of the floss or one strand of the braid to work the cross-stitches over two threads of the fabric. Work the blended needle stitches and the straight stitches as specified in the key *right*. Use one ply of floss or one strand of braid to work the backstitches. Refer to the diagrams on *page 100* to work the lazy daisy stitches, French knots, and couching stitches as specified in the key.

With raw edges even and right sides together, pin the lace to the edges of the napkin. Sew together ⅜" from the edges. Press the edges under ⅜"; blindstitch the raw edges in place.

ANGEL TABLE RUNNER

As shown on page 94, the finished table runner measures 20×36".

Fabric and Thread

24×40" piece of 25-count mushroom Lugana fabric

20×36" piece of tan lining fabric

Cotton embroidery floss in colors listed in the key on *page 101*

Kreinik #8 braid in colors listed in the key on *page 101*

Blending filament in colors listed in the key on *page 101*

Seed beads in colors listed in the key on *page 101*

Supplies

Needle; embroidery hoop

3⅔ yards of 1"-wide metallic gold flat lace

3⅔ yards of ⅛"-wide metallic red flat trim

Matching sewing threads

Instructions

Zigzag-stitch or overcast the edges of the Lugana fabric to prevent fraying. Find the vertical center of the chart and the vertical center of the fabric. Measure 7" from the bottom of the fabric's vertical center; begin stitching the bottom row of the center bottom snowflake motif there.

Use three plies of floss or one strand of the braid to work the cross-stitches over two threads of the fabric. Work the blended-needle stitches, satin stitches, and straight stitches as specified in the key on *page 101*. Work the backstitches using *Continued*

NAPKIN

Anchor		DMC	
944	◉	869	Dark hazel
236	■	3799	Charcoal
373	⊞	3828	True hazel
	♡	002	HL Kreinik gold #8 braid

BLENDED NEEDLE

683	⬤	500	Blue green (2X) and
		009	HL Kreinik green blending filament (2X)
923	⊟	699	Christmas green (2X) and
		009	HL Kreinik green blending filament (2X)

BACKSTITCH

	╱	002	HL Kreinik gold #8 braid – instrument, gown (1X)
	╱	003	Kreinik red #8 braid – napkin (1X)
382	╱	3371	Black brown – all remaining backstitches (1X)

COUCHING

	╱	001	Kreinik silver #8 braid (1X) and
002		000	White (1X) – instrument strings

SATIN STITCH

373	╱	3828	True hazel – lips (2X)

STRAIGHT STITCH

403	╱	310	Black – instrument on napkin (2X)

LAZY DAISY

923	⟋	699	Christmas green – instrument (2X)

FRENCH KNOT

403	●	310	Black – instrument on napkin (2X)

SEED BEADS

	●	03049	Mill Hill red seed beads

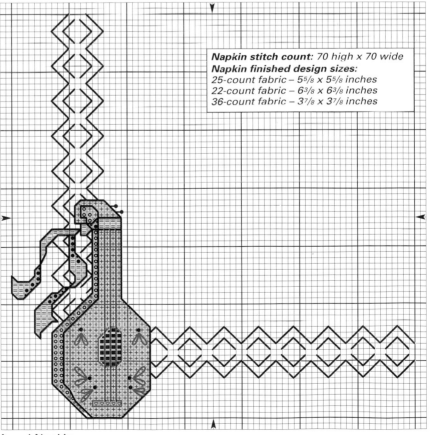

> **Napkin stitch count:** 70 high x 70 wide
> **Napkin finished design sizes:**
> 25-count fabric – 5⅝ x 5⅝ inches
> 22-count fabric – 6⅜ x 6⅜ inches
> 36-count fabric – 3⅞ x 3⅞ inches

Angel Napkin

Symbols of the Season

Table Runner stitch count: 114 high x 169 wide
Table Runner finished design sizes:
25-count fabric – 9 1/8 x 13 1/2 inches
22-count fabric – 10 3/8 x 15 3/8 inches
36-count fabric – 6 1/3 x 9 3/8 inches

Angel Table Runner

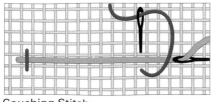

Couching Stitch

Satin Stitch

Lazy Daisy Stitch

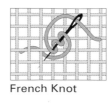

French Knot

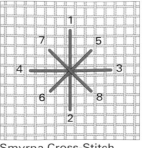

Smyrna Cross-Stitch

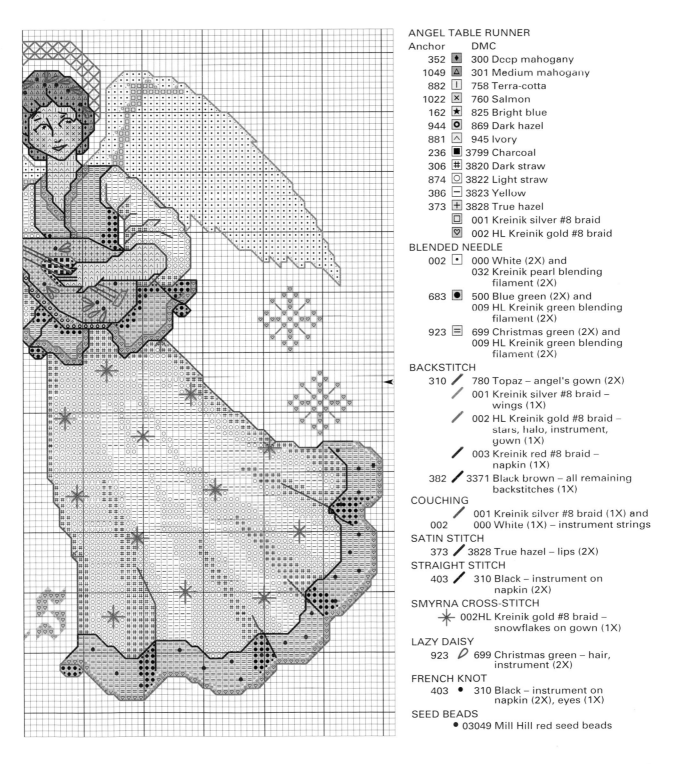

ANGEL TABLE RUNNER

Anchor		DMC
352	◆	300 Deep mahogany
1049	△	301 Medium mahogany
882	Ⅰ	758 Terra-cotta
1022	✕	760 Salmon
162	★	825 Bright blue
944	◉	869 Dark hazel
881	⋀	945 Ivory
236	■	3799 Charcoal
306	⊞	3820 Dark straw
874	◯	3822 Light straw
386	⊟	3823 Yellow
373	⊞	3828 True hazel
	☐	001 Kreinik silver #8 braid
	♡	002 HL Kreinik gold #8 braid

BLENDED NEEDLE
002	•	000 White (2X) and 032 Kreinik pearl blending filament (2X)
683	●	500 Blue green (2X) and 009 HL Kreinik green blending filament (2X)
923	⊟	699 Christmas green (2X) and 009 HL Kreinik green blending filament (2X)

BACKSTITCH
310	╱	780 Topaz – angel's gown (2X)
	╱	001 Kreinik silver #8 braid – wings (1X)
	╱	002 HL Kreinik gold #8 braid – stars, halo, instrument, gown (1X)
	╱	003 Kreinik red #8 braid – napkin (1X)
382	╱	3371 Black brown – all remaining backstitches (1X)

COUCHING
	╱	001 Kreinik silver #8 braid (1X) and
002		000 White (1X) – instrument strings

SATIN STITCH
373	╱	3828 True hazel – lips (2X)

STRAIGHT STITCH
403	╱	310 Black – instrument on napkin (2X)

SMYRNA CROSS-STITCH
	✳	002HL Kreinik gold #8 braid – snowflakes on gown (1X)

LAZY DAISY
923	⊘	699 Christmas green – hair, instrument (2X)

FRENCH KNOT
403	•	310 Black – instrument on napkin (2X), eyes (1X)

SEED BEADS
	•	03049 Mill Hill red seed beads

one ply of floss unless otherwise specified in the key.

Work the couching stitches, Smyrna cross-stitches, lazy daisy stitches, and French knots, referring to the diagrams *opposite,* and as specified in the key. Attach the seed beads with sewing thread. Turn the

fabric and repeat at the opposite end of the table runner.

Centering the design between the long edges, trim the Lugana fabric to measure 21×38½". With raw edges even and right sides together, baste the lace to the edges of the runner. With right sides together, sew the lining to the Lugana fabric along the

basting lines, leaving an opening to turn. Trim the seam allowances and clip the corners; turn right side out. Hand-sew the opening closed.

Position the flat red trim ⅛" from the edge of the Lugana fabric. Machine zigzag-stitch over the braid with red sewing thread.

POINSETTIA TOWEL AND NAPKIN

As shown on page 96.

Fabric and Thread
Purchased white towel with a
   13¾×3''-wide 14-count Aida
   cloth insert
Purchased 15×15'' 14-count white
   Royal Classic napkin
Cotton embroidery floss in colors
   listed in the key
DMC metallic gold thread

Supplies
Needle

Instructions
For the towel, find the center of the
chart and the center of the Aida cloth
insert; begin stitching there. Use
three plies of floss to work the cross-
stitches and three-quarter cross-
stitches. Use two plies of floss to
work the French-knot berries and
flower centers. Work the backstitches using one ply of floss unless otherwise specified. Press the finished
towel from the back.

For the napkin, measure 1⅜'' from
the left edge and ⅞'' from the bottom
on the left corner of the napkin;
begin stitching the bottom of the
poinsettia motif there. Use three
plies of floss to work the cross-
stitches and three-quarter cross-
stitches. Use two plies of floss to
work the French-knot flower center.
Work the backstitches using one ply
of floss unless otherwise specified.
Press the napkin from the back.

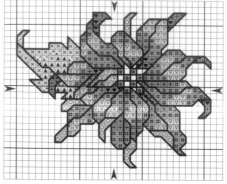

Poinsettia Napkin

POINSETTIA TOWEL AND NAPKIN

Anchor		DMC	
9046	+	321	Christmas red
923	▲	699	Christmas green
303	✳	742	Tangerine
1005	♥	816	Garnet
035	#	891	Carnation
205	✕	911	Emerald
203	╱	954	Nile green
033	▽	3706	Medium watermelon
031	◯	3708	Light watermelon

BACKSTITCH

382	╱	3371	Black brown – leaves and poinsettias (1X)
	╱	284	Metallic gold – hearts, stems of small leaves, and border (2X)

FRENCH KNOT

9046	●	321	Christmas red – berries (2X)
358	●	433	Chestnut – poinsettia centers (2X)

Towel stitch count: 29 high x 188 wide
Towel finished design sizes:
14-count fabric – 2⅛ x 13½ inches
11-count fabric – 2⅝ x 17⅛ inches
18-count fabric – 1⅝ x 10½ inches

Napkin stitch count: 25 high x 31 wide
Napkin finished design sizes:
14-count fabric – 1¾ x 2¼ inches
11-count fabric – 2¼ x 2⅞ inches
18-count fabric – 1⅜ x 1¾ inches

CHRISTMAS BELLS NAPKIN AND POT HOLDER

As shown on page 97.

Fabric and Thread
For each napkin
Purchased 15×15'' white 14-count
   Royal Classic napkin
For each pot holder
Purchased 8×8'' pot holder with a
   5×7'' white 14-count Aida insert
Cotton embroidery floss in colors
   listed in the key *opposite*
DMC metallic gold thread

Supplies
Needle

Instructions
For the napkin, measure ⅞'' from the
bottom and 1⅜'' from the right edge
of the napkin; begin stitching the
bottom row of the bell chart there.
For the pot holder, find the center of
the chart and the center of the Aida
cloth insert; begin stitching there.

Use three plies of floss to work
the cross-stitches. Work the straight
stitches on the leaves of the pot
holder as specified in the key. Work
the backstitches as specified in the
key. Referring to the diagrams *opposite*, work the Smyrna cross-stitches
on the napkin and the Algerian eyelets on the pot holder as specified in
the key. For the Algerian eyelets,
give each stitch a gentle tug to open
a small hole. Press the finished
pieces from the back.

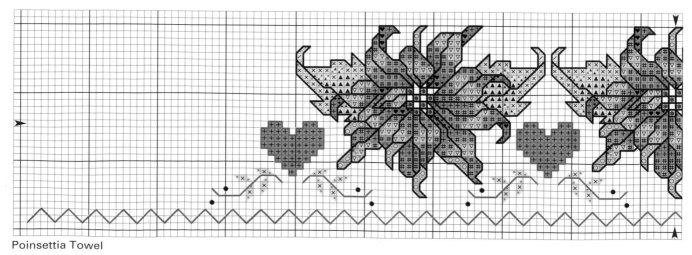

Poinsettia Towel

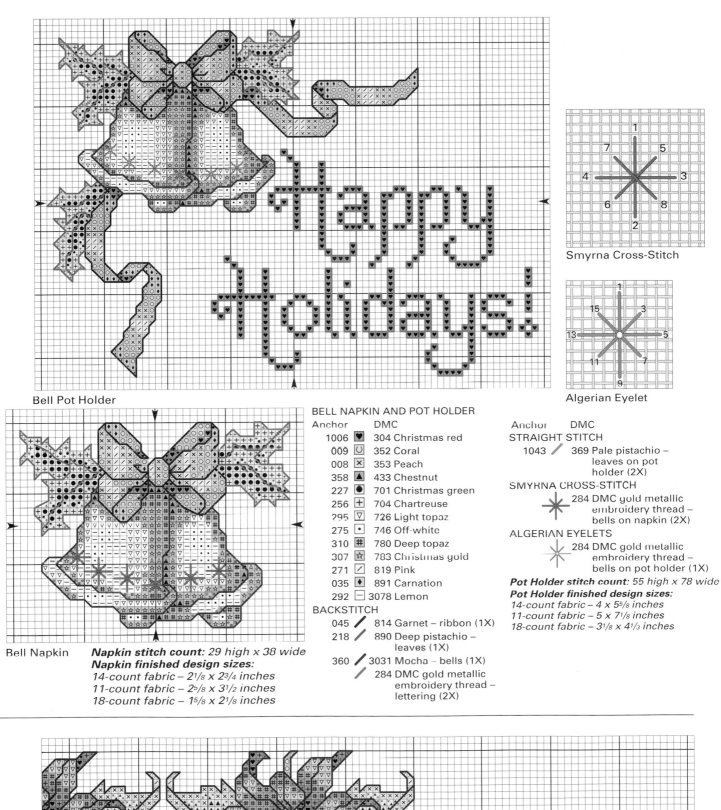

Bell Pot Holder

Smyrna Cross-Stitch

Algerian Eyelet

Bell Napkin

BELL NAPKIN AND POT HOLDER

Anchor		DMC	
1006	♥	304	Christmas red
009	◡	352	Coral
008	✕	353	Peach
358	▲	433	Chestnut
227	●	701	Christmas green
256	+	704	Chartreuse
295	▽	726	Light topaz
275	·	746	Off-white
310	#	780	Deep topaz
307	☆	783	Christmas gold
271	∕	819	Pink
035	◆	891	Carnation
292	⊟	3078	Lemon

BACKSTITCH

045	∕	814	Garnet – ribbon (1X)
218	∕	890	Deep pistachio – leaves (1X)
360	∕	3031	Mocha – bells (1X)
	∕	284	DMC gold metallic embroidery thread – lettering (2X)

Anchor		DMC	

STRAIGHT STITCH

1043	∕	369	Pale pistachio – leaves on pot holder (2X)

SMYRNA CROSS-STITCH

✳	284	DMC gold metallic embroidery thread – bells on napkin (2X)

ALGERIAN EYELETS

✳	284	DMC gold metallic embroidery thread – bells on pot holder (1X)

Pot Holder stitch count: 55 high x 78 wide
Pot Holder finished design sizes:
14-count fabric – 4 x 5⅝ inches
11-count fabric – 5 x 7⅛ inches
18-count fabric – 3⅛ x 4⅓ inches

Napkin stitch count: 29 high x 38 wide
Napkin finished design sizes:
14-count fabric – 2⅛ x 2¾ inches
11-count fabric – 2⅝ x 3½ inches
18-count fabric – 1⅝ x 2⅛ inches

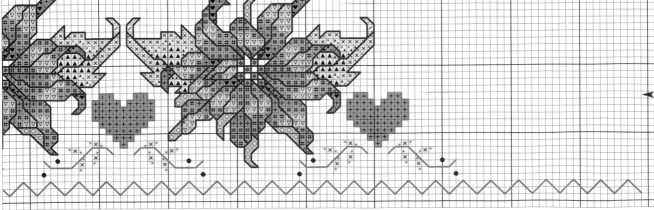

ALL HEARTS COME HOME SAMPLER

As shown on page 98.

Fabric and Thread
16×13" piece of 25-count cream-
and-gold Lugana fabric
#5 ecru pearl cotton
Rainbow Gallery Nordic Gold Pale
gold thread

Supplies
Needle
Needlework frame

Instructions
Zigzag-stitch or overcast the edges of the fabric to prevent fraying. Measure 3½" from both edges of the corner on the right-hand side of the fabric; begin working the first satin stitch there (*see the slender arrow on the chart*). **Note:** *Each square on the chart equals two threads of fabric.*

Row 1: Use one strand of pearl cotton to work the satin-stitch stars. Referring to Step 1 of the Needleweaving diagram, *right,* cut away the threads for the wrapped bar areas. Using one strand of Rainbow Gallery thread and referring to the Woven Bars with Adjoining Wrap diagram, *far right,* wrap the thread around two threads of the fabric to make the first bar.

Bring the needle under the adjacent two threads and then back up. Bring the needle under, and then back over the wrapped bar. Continue in this manner to make three more adjoining wraps. Then, wrap the remainder of the second bar. Repeat the wrapping and joining throughout the entire area. Work the diamond eyelet stitches using one strand of Rainbow Gallery thread and referring to the diagram, *lower right.*

Row 2: Work the satin-stitch trees and straight-stitch trunks using one strand of Rainbow Gallery thread.

Row 3: Referring to the Kloster Block diagram, *far right,* and working from the top of the heart to the bottom, use one strand of pearl cotton

to satin-stitch the Kloster blocks. Cut away the threads for the open squares and the dove's eye squares. Using one strand of Rainbow Gallery thread, work the needleweaving with dove's eye. Use one strand of the Rainbow Gallery thread to work the lettering.

Row 4: Use one strand of pearl cotton to satin-stitch the flowers. Using one strand of Rainbow Gallery thread, straight-stitch the leaves and the flower centers.

Row 5: Use one strand of pearl cotton to work the Kloster blocks. Cut away the threads for the open squares and the dove's eye squares. Using one strand of Rainbow Gallery thread, work the needle-weaving with dove's eye. Use one strand of Rainbow Gallery thread to satin-stitch the hearts and to backstitch. Press the finished stitchery from the back. Mat and frame the piece as desired.

ALL HEARTS COME HOME
SATIN STITCH
— Ecru #5 pearl cotton
/ ND1 Rainbow Gallery
Nordic Gold thread
BACKSTITCH
/ ND1 Rainbow Gallery
Nordic Gold thread
STRAIGHT STITCH
| ND1 Rainbow Gallery
Nordic Gold thread
DIAMOND EYELET STITCH
* ND1 Rainbow Gallery
Nordic Gold thread
NEEDLEWEAVING WITH DOVE'S EYE
ND1 Rainbow Gallery
Nordic Gold thread
WOVEN BARS WITH ADJOINING WRAP
ND1 Rainbow Gallery
Nordic Gold thread

Stitch count: *100 high x 70 wide*
Finished design sizes:
22-count fabric – 9¼ x 6⅜ inches
25-count fabric – 7½ x 5¼ inches
28-count fabric – 7¼ x 5 inches

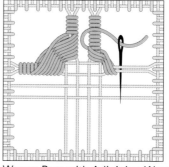
Woven Bars with Adjoining Wrap

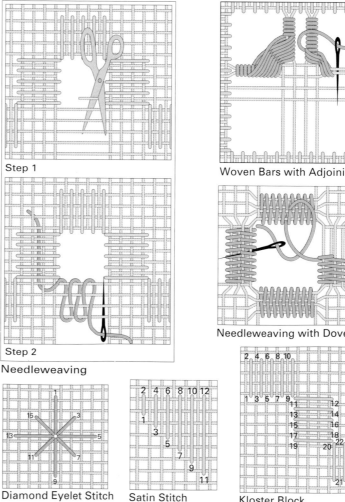
Step 1

Step 2
Needleweaving

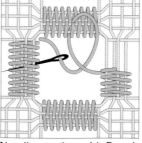
Needleweaving with Dove's Eye

Diamond Eyelet Stitch

Satin Stitch

Kloster Block

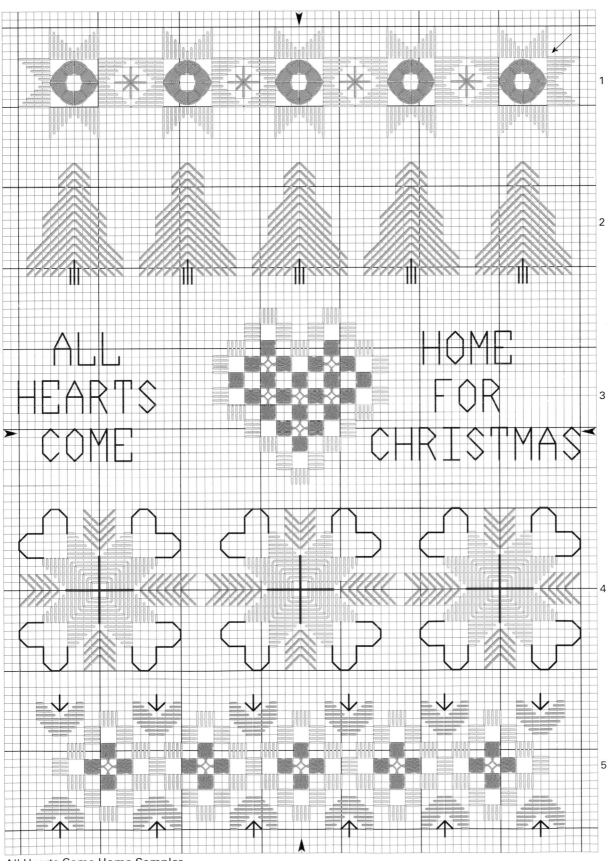

All Hearts Come Home Sampler

Dressed in
HOLIDAY
Style

Set the holidays aglow with festive fashions for girls of all ages. Here and on the following pages, we showcase an elegant silk blouse abloom with Christmas flowers and a stunning brocade-like evening bag for the grownups, and two sweet garment accents—a kitty-motif collar and a teddy bear-design vest—for the little girls.

Express your creativity by wearing your art on your sleeve! This beautifully embroidered silk blouse welcomes Christmas, styled with traditional colors of red and green silk ribbons, metallic gold braid, and a classic accent-trim of beads. Echoing motifs at the cuffs coordinate with the flattering collar.

Designer Alice Okon from Missoula, Montana, designed the motifs for all to enjoy stitching—experienced stitchers as well as those who are new to the classic art of ribbon embroidery. Most of the stitches used in this design are simple variations on crewel-embroidery stitches and the clear diagrams on page 112 make completing this blouse a cinch.

DRESSED IN HOLIDAY STYLE

Designer Ruth Schmuff from Randallstown, Maryland, designed a beautiful holiday accessory to accompany us on holiday visits, to company parties, or to an intimate dinner for two.

Consisting of only two different kinds of thread, ecru embroidery floss and metallic gold braid, the graceful fleur-de-lis motifs on mushroom Lugana fabric create the rich appearance of brocade. The fleur-de-lis is an artistic representation of the iris that dates back to the medieval days and was most frequently used in heraldry.

Two rows of Algerian eyelets accent the gathered top of the bag that's cinched together by ready-made gold cord. A dazzling gold tassel accented with pearl trim frivolously dangles from the gathered bottom of the evening bag.

A simple Lugana-fabric vest or bolero jacket embroidered entirely with this stylish pattern would form an absolutely stunning ensemble when paired with the bag.

DRESSED IN HOLIDAY STYLE

Grandma's little angel, *opposite,* is proof positive that our darling kitty collar will be a hit with the girls on your gift list. The mischievous kitten in the design appears to have plucked a shiny ball from the Christmas tree with its tiny furry paw. Barbara Sestok from Germantown, New York, used fine 32-count cherub-pink Royal Danish linen for this heirloom garment accent.

For casual holiday dress, your young one will enjoy this tree-trimming-Teddy vest. Virginia Soskin from Ormond Beach, Florida, designed the helpful bruins for stitching on 14-count country-oatmeal Royal Classic fabric. We finished ours into a size 5 vest using a commercial pattern, but this motif fits nicely on any garment. Try stitching it for a baby's bib, or mat and frame it for your child's room. To flop the image for the opposite side of the vest, stand a mirror next to the chart—you'll get a perfect mirror image.

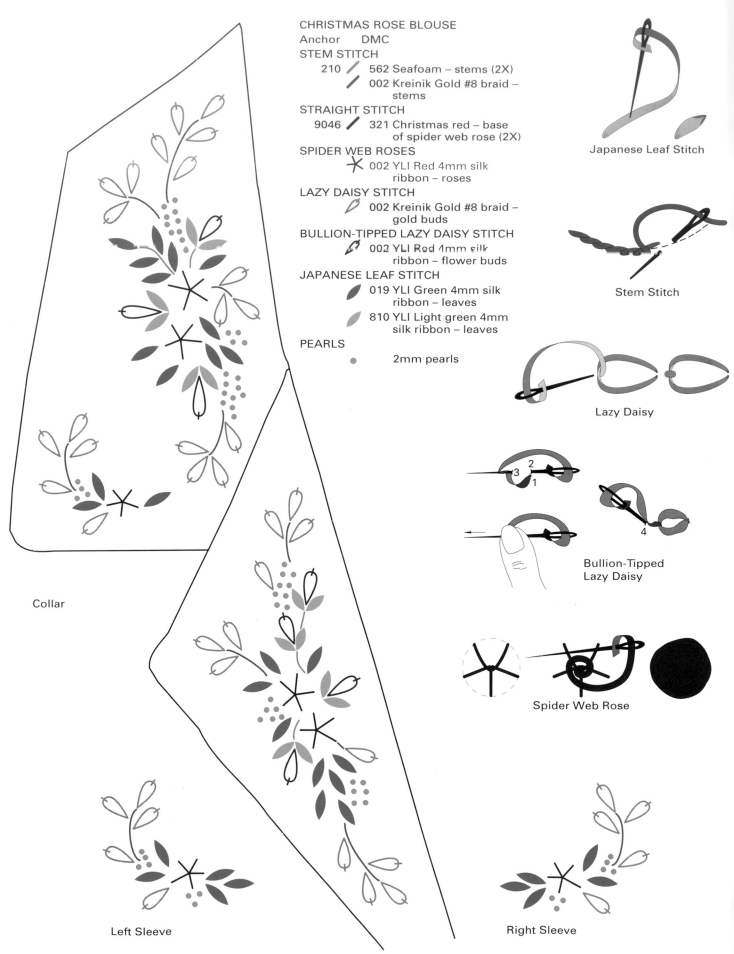

CHRISTMAS ROSE BLOUSE

Anchor   DMC

STEM STITCH

    210   562 Seafoam – stems (2X)

            002 Kreinik Gold #8 braid – stems

STRAIGHT STITCH

    9046   321 Christmas red – base of spider web rose (2X)

SPIDER WEB ROSES

       002 YLI Red 4mm silk ribbon – roses

LAZY DAISY STITCH

       002 Kreinik Gold #8 braid – gold buds

BULLION-TIPPED LAZY DAISY STITCH

       002 YLI Red 4mm silk ribbon – flower buds

JAPANESE LEAF STITCH

       019 YLI Green 4mm silk ribbon – leaves

       810 YLI Light green 4mm silk ribbon – leaves

PEARLS

       2mm pearls

Japanese Leaf Stitch

Stem Stitch

Lazy Daisy

Bullion-Tipped Lazy Daisy

Spider Web Rose

Collar

Left Sleeve

Right Sleeve

DRESSED IN HOLIDAY STYLE

EMBROIDERED BLOUSE

As shown on pages 107.

Fabric and Thread
Purchased ecru silk blouse with a notch collar
Cotton embroidery floss in colors listed in the key
#8 Kreinik (002) gold braid
4mm silk ribbon in colors listed in the key

Supplies
Tracing paper
Iron-on transfer pen
Sharp needle
120—2mm pearls

Instructions
Place tracing paper over the patterns. Trace the designs with an iron-on transfer pen. To flop the collar pattern for the other side of the collar, trace it with an ink pen or pencil, then turn the tracing paper over and trace over the drawn lines with the iron-on transfer pen.

It's not necessary to go over each symbol in full as printed in the patterns, just indicate the vine by a line, use a small straight line to indicate each leaf and a small circle to indicate each flower. You don't want to make any large marks that will be difficult to cover with the embroidery. Refer to the patterns, and the photograph on *page 107* as you stitch.

Place the traced patterns on the appropriate areas of the blouse. Iron the markings onto the blouse following the manufacturer's instructions.

Use a sharp needle to work the embroidery stitches—a tapestry needle could make snags or runs in the blouse fabric. Work all the stem stitches first, using two plies of floss or one strand of braid. Work the lazy daisy stitches using one strand of braid and referring to the diagram. Using one strand of ribbon and referring to the diagrams work the ribbon embroidery stitches. Attach the pearls with two plies of ecru floss. Place the finished blouse facedown on a soft towel and carefully press from the back.

ELEGANT BAG

As shown on page 108.

Fabric and Thread
22×28" piece of 25-count mushroom Lugana fabric
Kreinik 002 gold #8 braid
Ecru cotton embroidery floss
Ecru #8 pearl cotton
14½×21½" piece of gold lamé fabric

Supplies
Needle
Embroidery hoop
Air-soluble fabric marking pen
1½ yards of ⅜"-diameter metallic gold cord
Matching sewing thread

For the tassel:
3 skeins medium old gold (DMC 729) floss
2 spools of Kreinik 2000 gold Ombre thread
Air-soluble fabric marking pen
One ¾"-diameter wooden bead
4×4-inch piece of cardboard
¼ yard of 2mm pearls-by-the-yard trim
Crafts glue

Instructions
Zigzag-stitch or overcast the edges of the Lugana fabric to prevent fraying. Find the center of the chart and the center of the fabric, count eight threads up and to the left, and begin stitching there. Use three plies of floss, one strand of braid, or one strand of pearl cotton to work the cross-stitches over two threads of the fabric. Work the backstitches using one strand of the braid. Referring to the diagram on *page 114,* work the Algerian eyelets using one strand of pearl cotton and giving each stitch a gentle tug to open a small hole. Use the air-soluble fabric marking pen to mark the position of the buttonholes as indicated on the chart.

Centering the design, trim the stitched fabric to measure 14½×21½", and use the stitchery as a pattern to cut a matching lining from the gold lamé fabric. All measurements include a ½" seam allowance. Work the marked button-hole stitches on each side of the bag. Cut the buttonholes open. With right sides together and raw edges even, sew the center 14½" centerback seam of the stitched fabric.

Sew gathering threads ½" and ¼" along the bottom edge of the bag. Pull the gathering threads tightly and secure the thread ends.

Sew the centerback seam of the gold lamé lining fabric, leaving an opening in the seam for turning. Sew gathering threads ½" and ¼" along the bottom edge of the lining. Pull the gathering threads tightly and secure. With right sides together and raw edges even, sew the top of the purse to the top of the lining. Turn right side out; press. Whip-stitch the lining opening closed.

For the casing, machine-stitch through both layers of fabric, 1" and 1⅝" from the top edge of the purse. Cut gold cord into two equal lengths. Touch the ends of each cord with glue to prevent fraying; let the glue dry. Thread one length of the gold cord through the casing on each side of the bag. Knot the cord ends together on each side of the bag.

For the tassel, cut two 6-inch lengths of medium old gold floss (DMC 729); set aside. Bundle one 6-ply strand of medium old gold floss (DMC 729) and 2 strands of the Ombre thread, and wrap around the 4×4" piece of cardboard 48 times.

Firmly tie the wrapped strands together at one edge of the cardboard using one 6" length of floss. Cut the threads at the opposite edge of the cardboard. Embed the wooden bead inside the thread bundle directly under the tied part. Tie the remaining 6" piece of floss around the thread bundle below the covered bead. Wrap the pearl trim below the covered bead; secure both ends of the pearl trim. Tack the tassel to the center bottom of the purse; trim the tassel ends.

Dressed in Holiday Style

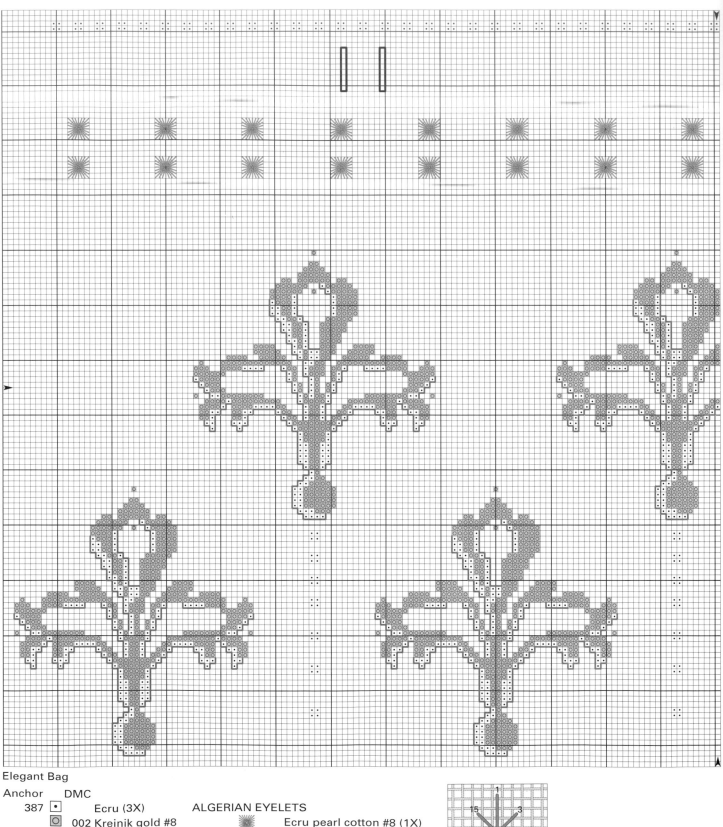

Elegant Bag

Anchor		DMC	
387	•		Ecru (3X)
	◎	002	Kreinik gold #8 braid (1X)

BACKSTITCH

| | / | 002 | Kreinik gold #8 braid (1X) |

ALGERIAN EYELETS

※ Ecru pearl cotton #8 (1X)

Stitch count: 134 high x 257 wide

Finished design sizes:
25-count fabric – 10¾ x 20½ inches
22-count fabric – 12¼ x 23⅜ inches
36-count fabric – 7½ x 14¼ inches

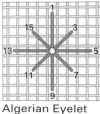

Algerian Eyelet

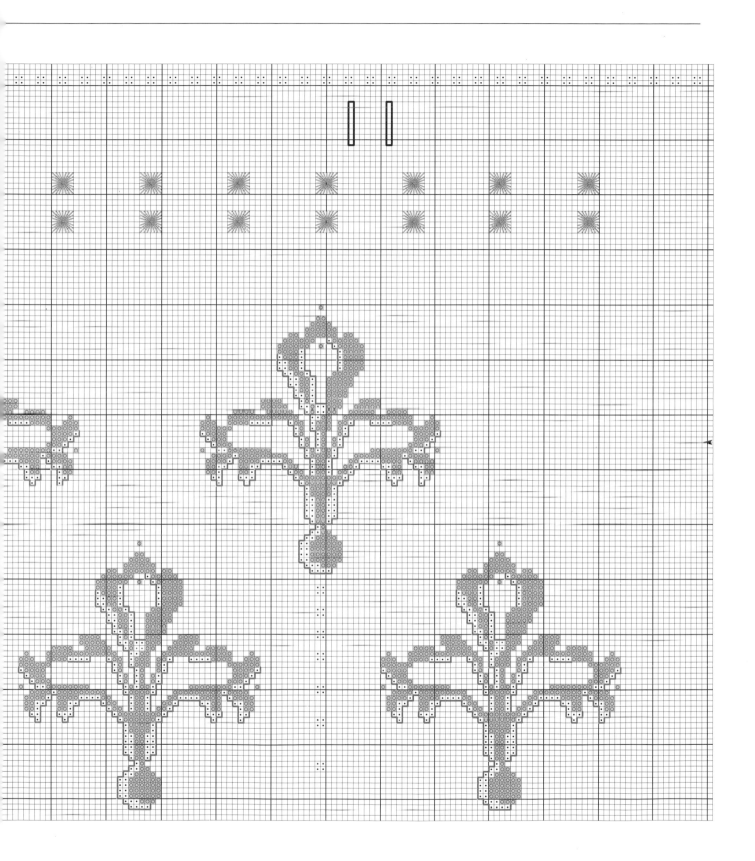

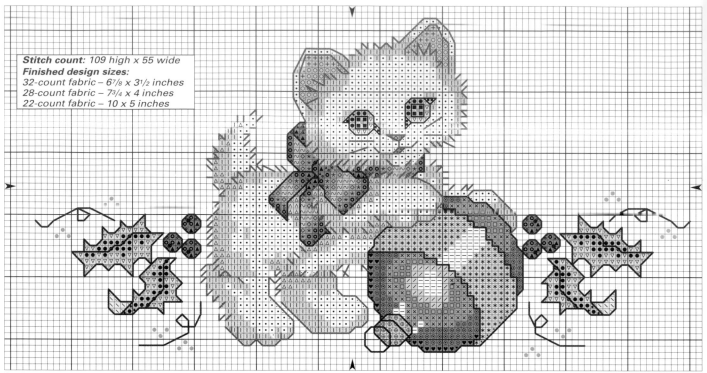

Stitch count: 109 high x 55 wide
Finished design sizes:
32-count fabric – 6⁷⁄₈ x 3¹⁄₂ inches
28-count fabric – 7³⁄₄ x 4 inches
22-count fabric – 10 x 5 inches

Christmas Kitten Collar

CHRISTMAS KITTEN COLLAR

As shown on page 110.

Fabric and Thread
For a child's size 4
20×20" piece of 32-count cherub-
  pink Royal Danish linen
18×20" piece of white fabric
Lightweight fusible interfacing
Cotton embroidery floss in colors
  listed in the key
Kreinik #8 braid in colors listed in
  the key
Blending filament in colors listed
  in the key

Supplies
Tracing paper
Needle
Embroidery hoop
Mill Hill 40557 gold petite
  seed beads
Air-soluble fabric marking pen
1¹⁄₂ yards of ³⁄₄"-wide flat white lace
24" length of ¹⁄₁₆"-wide white
  satin ribbon
Matching sewing thread

Instructions
Fold the tracing paper in half.
Transfer the front collar pattern
opposite onto one half of the tracing
paper. Unfold the tracing paper and
continue tracing the back collar pattern on the other half of the paper.
Cut out the pattern; set aside.

Zigzag-stitch or overcast the
edges of the linen to prevent fraying.
Find the vertical center of the fabric
and the vertical center of the chart.
Measure up 3¹⁄₄" from the bottom of
the vertical center of the fabric;
begin stitching the bottom row of the
kitty's paw there. Use three plies of
floss to work the cross-stitches over
two threads of the fabric. Work the
blended-needle stitches using two
plies of floss and one strand of
blending filament. Work the backstitches using one ply of floss unless
otherwise specified in the key. Work
the straight stitches using one ply of
floss. Use one ply of floss to work
the French knots wrapping the
thread one time around the needle
for the eye highlight and two times
for the berry details. Attach the seed
beads using one ply of matching
floss. Press the finished stitchery
from the back.

Position the tracing paper pattern
over the stitched fabric with the
design centered side-to-side and the
bottom of the design ³⁄₄" from the
Continued

CHRISTMAS KITTEN COLLAR

Anchor		DMC	
002	⊡	000	White
403	■	310	Black
9046	◉	321	Christmas red
009	+	352	Coral
398	△	415	Light pearl gray
227	●	701	Christmas green
256	▽	704	Chartreuse
234	I	762	Pale pearl gray
043	▲	815	Garnet
035	✳	3705	Dark watermelon
033	◈	3706	Medium watermelon
1020	∼	3713	Salmon
278	◺	3819	Moss green
9575	◯	3824	Melon
	⊕	001	Kreinik #8 silver braid
	✳	002	Kreinik #8 gold braid

BLENDED NEEDLE

002	⊟	000	White (2X) and 032 Kreinik pearl blending filament (1X)
9046	◉	321	Christmas red (2X) and 003HL Kreinik red blending filament (1X)
043	♥	815	Garnet (2X) and 003HL Kreinik red blending filament (1X)
035	☒	3705	Dark watermelon (2X) and 003HL Kreinik red blending filament (1X)
033	☐	3706	Medium watermelon (2X) and 003HL Kreinik red blending filament (1X)
1020	⊠	3713	Salmon (2X) and 032 Kreinik pearl blending filament (1X)

BACKSTITCH

403	╱	310	Black–eye
043	╱	815	Garnet–bow, ornament, berries (1X); scroll (2X)
382	╱	3371	Black brown–leaves, ornament
400	╱	3799	Pewter–kitten

STRAIGHT STITCH

400	╱	3799	Pewter–whiskers

FRENCH KNOT

002	•	000	White–eye
382	●	3371	Black brown–berries

MILL HILL BEADS

●	40557	Gold petite glass bead

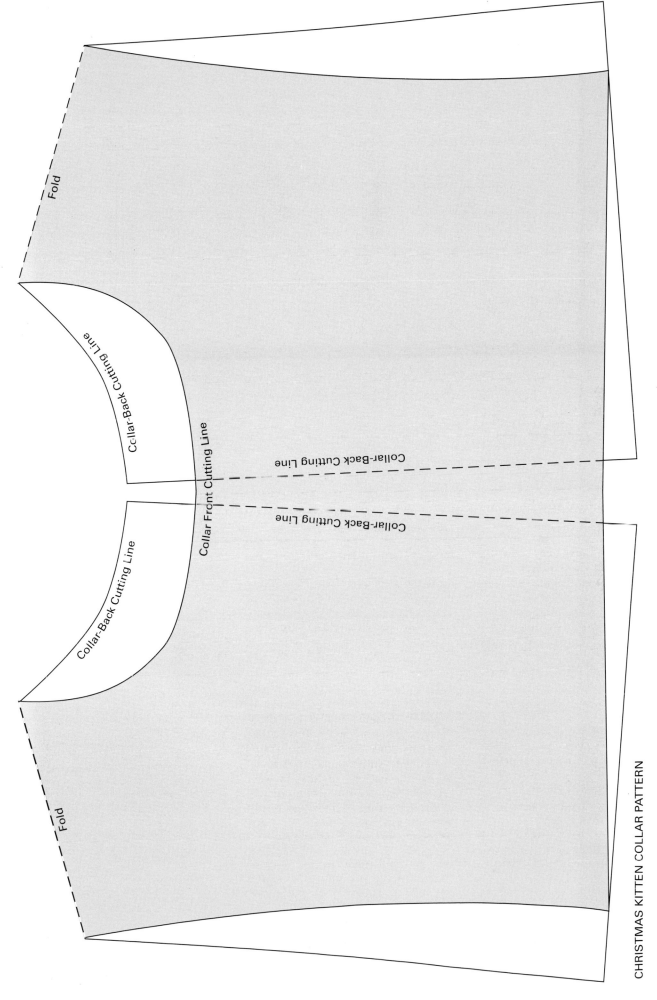

Fold

Collar-Back Cutting Line

Collar-Back Cutting Line

Collar Front Cutting Line

Collar-Back Cutting Line

Collar-Back Cutting Line

Fold

CHRISTMAS KITTEN COLLAR PATTERN

117

bottom of the collar front. Use the air-soluble fabric marking pen to draw the collar outline on the fabric. Fuse the interfacing to the back of the fabric following the manufacturer's instructions.

Cut out the collar ½" beyond the marked line. Use the stitched collar as a pattern to cut one lining piece from the white fabric. Sew all seams with right sides together unless otherwise specified.

Baste the lace around the collar with raw edges even and right sides together. Sew a 12" length of ribbon to each top back corner of the stitched collar. Sew the collar to the lining along the basting lines being careful not to catch the ribbons in the seams. Leave an opening at the center back for turning. Trim the seam allowances and turn the collar right side out. Press the collar carefully. Slip-stitch the opening closed.

TREE TRIMMIN' TEDDY VEST

As shown on page 111.

Fabric and Floss
60"-wide, 14-count country oatmeal Royal Classic fabric in the amount specified on the pattern envelope
Red lining fabric in the amount specified on the pattern envelope (optional)
Cotton embroidery floss in colors listed in the key

Supplies
Purchased vest pattern (we used Simplicity #9778 size 5)
Light-color fabric marking pencil
Needle; embroidery hoop
3 yards of ¼"-wide red flat braid trim
Matching sewing thread

Instructions
Zigzag-stitch or overcast the edges of the Royal Classic fabric to prevent fraying. Use the fabric marking pencil to trace the outlines (with seam allowances) of the vest front pieces onto the Royal Classic fabric, allowing 2" between outlines. Omit any

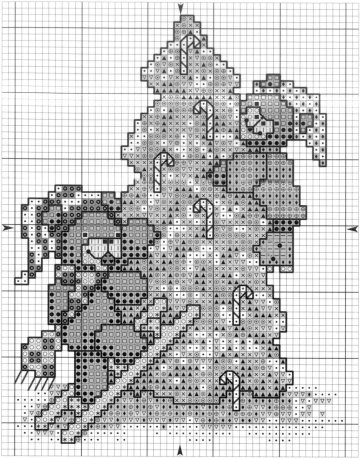

Tree Trimmin' Teddy Vest

pockets or pocket flaps, but allow space for back ties and facings if included in the pattern instructions.

For the right vest front, make two marks 1½" from each edge at one corner of a piece of paper. Center the marked corner of the paper over the curved corner outline marked on the fabric, aligning the 1½" marks with the outline. Begin stitching the right stitch of the bottom row of the chart there. Use three plies of the floss to work the cross-stitches. Work the backstitches using one ply of floss unless otherwise specified in the key. Work the French knots and straight stitches as specified in the key. Stitch the left vest front as directed for the right front, working the chart in reverse.

Redraw the vest outlines. Cut out the vest fronts, vest back and lining, and facings and back ties if included. Sew the vest together following the pattern instructions. Sew the red braid trim along all edges of the vest.

TREE TRIMMIN' TEDDY VEST

Anchor		DMC	
002	•	000	White
342	—	211	Lavender
403	■	310	Black
1046	●	435	Chestnut
362	▢	437	Tan
1005	♥	498	Christmas red
683	▲	500	Blue green
098	♦	553	Violet
210	✕	562	Seafoam
046	◉	666	Red
891	○	676	Light old gold
886	❘	677	Pale old gold
901	✳	680	Dark old gold
144	▽	800	Delft blue
928	⊕	3761	Sky blue
188	⊙	3814	Aquamarine

BACKSTITCH

891	╱	666	Red—candy cane stripes
360	╱	3031	Mocha—all remaining stitches

STRAIGHT STITCH

891	╱	666	Red—scarf fringe
886	╱	676	Pale old gold— boot laces

FRENCH KNOT

360	•	3031	Mocha – faces and boots

GET PROFESSIONAL-LOOKING RESULTS

Even though the cross-stitch technique is relatively straightforward, all good stitchers take a few basic steps to ensure the best results: They correctly position the stitchery on the fabric, they neatly begin and end threads, and they properly form the stitches whether they're adjacent or separated. Here's how to make sure your work is as attractive and durable as that of any expert.

Preparing the Fabric

Preparing the fabric for stitching involves three basic steps: pressing the fabric, binding the edges, and basting. Even-weave fabric often is sold in small pieces wrapped in plastic. Though this keeps the fabric clean, the resulting creases sometimes are difficult to remove.

Pressing out the creases and folds before stitching lessens the pressing required after the fabric is stitched. (Heavy pressing over stitched areas can flatten stitches and alter the color and appearance of the design.) To remove the creases, mist the fabric lightly and press with a warm iron. For stubborn folds, saturate the fabric or cover it with a wet press cloth before ironing. Or try applying a weak solution of vinegar and water to the creases.

All fabrics unravel along the cut edges while being stitched; some weaves unravel more easily than others. The raveled threads not only diminish the size of the background fabric, but they're also bothersome when they become tangled with the embroidery threads. Binding the edges of the fabric will eliminate raveling. The best way to bind the fabric edges is to machine-zigzag-stitch along the raw edges.

Regardless of the size or complexity of the stitchery, it's a good idea to add basted lines to the background to position it correctly. Depending on the nature of the chart, basted lines can be added in various ways. For a single motif, merely basting the horizontal and vertical centers is sufficient. These lines are essential for stitching a chart divided into quadrants. For complicated designs, you may wish to baste horizontal and vertical lines every 10 stitches to correspond to the bolder lines of a chart.

Flosses and yarns require less preparation than the fabric, but for large or complicated projects, a little advance work can eliminate later confusion. Floss caddies are available at needlework-supply outlets. These enable a stitcher to store cut lengths of thread. They also keep the individual thread colors separated, which can be important when you work with closely shaded colors of thread.

When working with many colors, it's handy to make a small card of threads before beginning. Jot the color names and numbers on an index card; tape a snippet of thread next to the corresponding label to use as a reference while stitching.

Making the Cross-Stitches

To make a cross-stitch, pull a threaded needle from the wrong side of the fabric in a lower corner of the stitch. Carry the needle to the opposite upper corner of the stitch and insert it through the fabric from front to back. This makes the first half of the cross-stitch.

(*Note: The number of threads of fabric a stitch is worked over will vary from project to project. Refer to each project's instructions for directions.*)

To complete the stitch, make another stitch between opposite corners to cover the first half. The first half of the cross-stitch may be worked from lower left to upper right or from lower right to upper left. In either case, make sure that all of the stitches are crossed in the same direction. This becomes especially important when you're working a quadrant pattern and have to turn the work at right angles.

Beginning and Ending Threads

The best way to begin a cross-stitch is by using a waste knot, a temporary knot that will be clipped when no longer necessary. To begin, knot the end of your thread. Insert the needle into the right side of the fabric about 4 inches from the first cross-stitch. Bring the needle up through the fabric and work the first series of cross-stitches. Stitch until the thread is used up or until the area using this color is complete.

To end a working thread, slip the needle under the previously stitched threads on the wrong side of the fabric for 1 to 1½ inches. Clip the thread. Turn the piece to the right side and clip the beginning knot. Rethread the needle with the excess floss, and pull the thread through to the wrong side of the stitchery. Finish the thread as directed *above*.

If you're working in areas that use a variety of thread colors (for example, a multicolored bouquet of tiny flowers), you may not wish to begin and end the thread for each flower or leaf. In these instances, carry the thread across the back of the fabric. To secure the thread, slip the threaded needle under previously stitched crosses.

When carrying threads across the back of the fabric, tension is important. If your tension is too tight, the fabric tends to bunch up; if the tension is too loose, the back becomes messy and threads may tangle and twist or leave a shadow on the front of the work.

Using the Charts

Most stitchers are accustomed to stitching from charts. The charts in this book feature symbols, each one representing a cross-stitch worked in a particular color. The symbols are coded in a color key adjacent to the chart. Each symbol on the grid represents one cross-stitch, unless specified otherwise in the instructions. Because many of the patterns in this book are too large to fit on one page, individual charts may have to be pieced together to form the complete pattern.

Correcting Mistakes

Regardless of the complexity of a design or the skill of stitcher, mistakes are inevitable. What to do about them depends largely upon their magnitude, when they're discovered, and what's necessary to correct them.

Small errors, such as working one or two additional stitches within a shaded area or stitching the end of a leaf so that it points in the wrong direction, usually will go unnoticed. Some areas of stitching, however, must be perfect or the rest of the design won't look right. When you've stitched around the border of a sampler, for example, and the corners don't align, there's little choice but to find the error and rework the stitches.

To remove stitches, use a pair of sharp scissors with tiny blades. Working from the back side, carefully snip away the threads and discard them. Use a pair of tweezers to pluck out stubborn threads.

ASSEMBLE AND DISPLAY YOUR WORK

Careful finishing adds to the beauty of a cross-stitch design. Cleaning, pressing, and assembling a stitchery are simple steps that also will protect and preserve your work for many years to come.

Cleaning

Even the most fastidious stitchers still will need to clean a completed cross-stitch piece. A stitchery may appear clean, but oils from your hands accumulate on fabric and thread and eventually will soil them.

Cross-stitched pieces may be dry-cleaned or washed by hand. One advantage to hand-laundering is that it will remove hoop marks more effectively than dry-cleaning.

To launder a stitchery, thoroughly dissolve some detergent in cold water. Add the stitchery and gently squeeze the suds through the fabric. Rinse well in cold water (change the water rather than holding the fabric under a faucet); continue until no soap remains.

Remove excess water by rolling the piece in a towel. Don't wring the fabric; wrinkles will be difficult to remove.

Place the fabric facedown on a smooth towel (terry-cloth towels may leave marks). Iron the fabric until it's dry. Ironing, rather than air-drying, gives the fabric more body. Never dry cross-stitched fabric in a dryer.

Finishing the Edges

Stitcheries intended to be used flat, such as table covers or doilies, simply require hemming so the edges won't ravel.

For a double-fold hem, turn under the raw edge to the wrong side approximately ⅛ inch then turn under ¼ inch. Finger-press the edges; baste. Hand-stitch with tiny stitches or machine-topstitch with matching thread.

To trim an edge with rickrack, mark the desired finished dimensions on the right side of the fabric. Center the rickrack on this line, and machine-topstitch along the center edge of the rickrack. Trim the raw edges of the fabric even with the outer points of the rickrack. Turn and press rickrack to the wrong side, allowing half of the rickrack to show past the edge. Topstitch the rickrack in place.

Making Pillows, Sachets, and Ornaments

Despite their difference in size, pillows, sachets, and ornaments are assembled in the same manner.

To assemble a pillow or ornament without adding trims to the edges, simply mark the finished size on the wrong side of the stitchery. Pin a piece of backing fabric to the stitchery, right sides facing. Stitch along the outline, leaving an opening for turning. Trim the seams, turn the work, and press. Stuff with fiberfill to the desired firmness. Slip-stitch the opening closed.

Making Ruffles and Piping

Ruffles and piping add a tailored touch to a three-dimensional shape. You can purchase ready-made piping and ruffles at fabric stores, but to perfectly match other fabrics and colors, make your own.

With striped or plaid fabric, cut the ruffle or piping strips on the straight grain or on the bias—the choice depends on the nature of the print. Cut plain fabric on the bias; the ruffles will be more graceful and the piping will be easier to shape. Crosswise-cut straight-grain strips are somewhat easier to handle than those cut lengthwise.

To make ruffles, cut fabric into strips that are twice the width of the finished size plus twice the width of the seam allowance. (Use ½-inch seam allowances for large items like pillows and ¼-inch seam allowances for smaller items.) The length of the strip should be at least twice the finished length of the edge it will be stitched to. Cut strips, seam the ends to form a circle, then fold it in half lengthwise, keeping raw edges even; press. Machine-stitch (on the longest stitch setting) two rows through both thicknesses; stitch one row directly on the seam line and the second row evenly between the first row and the raw edge. Pull the bobbin threads to gather.

For piping, fold a strip of fabric around the cording; baste the raw edges together. (Do not baste snugly against the cording at this point.) Trim the seam allowance to match that of the ruffle.

Applying Piping and Ruffles

It's easiest to apply piping and ruffles to the right side of the stitchery before further assembly. Cut away the excess fabric to form the same seam allowance as for the piping/ruffle. Pin the piping/ruffle to the right side of the work, keeping the raw edges even with the edge of the stitchery. The folded edge of the ruffle and the corded edge of the piping should face the center of the stitchery, with the raw edges of both facing outward. Be sure the ruffle's fullness is evenly distributed, with extra fullness at the corners to prevent the ruffle from cupping. Baste the piping/ruffle directly over the seam line.

Framing

Heirloom stitcheries and large samplers are best displayed in frames. Covering a stitchery with glass is a matter of personal preference, but glass must be held away from the fabric with spacers. (Moisture may be trapped and will condense on the inside of the glass; when fabric is placed against the glass, it can rot.)

Ready-made frames are widely available in a range of sizes and styles. When selecting a frame, choose one that's in keeping with the nature of your stitchery—a simple wooden frame might work best for a country-style sampler, just as a painted metal frame would better complement a contemporary stitchery.

Professional framing is another option. A frame shop will have more frames to select from, and a framer can add matting.

To mount a stitchery, cut a piece of ⅛- to ¼-inch-thick mounting board to the desired size. Pad the front of the board with quilt batting, if desired. Wrap the stitchery around the board. Temporarily insert pins into the edges of the board, starting at the center point of each side; add more pins, working toward the corners. Make sure the grainlines of the fabric run parallel to the board's edges.

With the piece facedown, fold the excess fabric to the wrong side; trim the excess, leaving approximately 1½ inches. Miter the corners, cutting away the excess fabric. Use a fabric glue stick to affix the fabric to the back of the board. When the glue is dry, remove the pins. Secure the board in the frame. Finish by gluing paper to the back edges of the frame.

CREATE YOUR OWN CROSS-STITCH DESIGNS

Even if designing isn't your forte, you still can create lovely stitcheries with a personal touch by collecting cross-stitch motifs and arranging them until you achieve a pleasing design. These tips will help you create cross-stitch originals for yourself, your family, and your friends.

Collecting the Patterns

Begin by browsing through current crafts books and magazines. Watch for needlepoint, filet crochet, and fair-isle knitting patterns, too, because they translate easily into cross-stitch designs.

Clip motifs you like, or copy them onto graph paper. Search for old pattern books and stitcheries at antique shops and garage sales. Look through coloring books and other children's books for design possibilities. Then convert them to cross-stitch patterns by laying the pictures atop a light box (or taping them to a window), placing graph paper over them, and charting the areas with symbols.

Organizing the Designs

Place the patterns between acetate sheets for protection, and store them in a ring binder. For your convenience and easy reference, divide the patterns into sections labeled by subject matter—alphabets, borders, animals, Christmas motifs, flowers, and any other subjects you like.

Charting the Patterns

As special occasions approach, pull out the binder and select appropriate motifs. If a name or message is included, chart it first; then place the motifs in a pleasing arrangement around the message.

It's easiest to design patterns with a repeat motif. For a pillow, start with a quarter of the total design; complete it by making mirror images in the remaining three sections. The pillow on *page 55* is an example of this kind of pattern.

Create a picture similarly, except design half of the chart and flop it to complete the mirror image.

To make a sampler, chart an alphabet, a message, and then your name. Select some of your favorite motifs, such as small flowers, hearts, or some interesting leaf patterns, and arrange them around your lettering. Then establish a simple border to hold your sampler together. Keep in mind that most samplers are very linear and need not be complex.

Stitching your Design

Remember that your design on graph paper won't be the finished size of your work; in most cases, the design will be considerably larger on paper. Determine the finished size of your stitchery before you purchase your materials or begin stitching the piece.

Count the number of stitches and empty spaces across both the width and the length of your chart. Then consider the stitching options: When you work on 14-count Aida cloth over one thread of the cloth, you'll have 14 stitches or spaces, or combinations of the two, for every inch of the stitching.

If you use Hardanger with 22 threads per inch and stitch over one thread, your finished piece will be considerably smaller than when you stitch on Aida cloth. Or you might stitch over two threads of the Hardanger; then your piece will be twice as large as one stitched over one thread of the same cloth.

The selection of the number of threads of embroidery floss—or the use of pearl cotton, Persian yarns, ribbons, or other yarns or threads—can affect the finished appearance and size of your stitched piece. Experiment with several possibilities before beginning your work.

Checkpoints In Your Stitching

As you work your cross-stitch project, it's wise to periodically check your work to avoid having to rip out mistakes. This is especially important when working with dark threads on light fabrics because dark threads may leave a stain after they've been removed.

Examine your work each time you complete a section of a design to make sure the cross-stitches are complete stitches and that the top stitch of each cross is worked in the same direction throughout.

When working a border design, stitch the basics (or the stitches with the lighter threads) of the border first to make sure your count is accurate, then complete the remaining portions of the border later.

MATERIALS FOR CROSS-STITCH

Counted cross-stitch remains the most popular form of needlework. Many stitchers like to work cross-stitch designs on different types of fabrics and use threads unlike those specified in the projects. Here's some information to help you understand the projects in this book and adapt them to your own special needs.

Cross-Stitch Fabrics

Work counted cross-stitch on any fabric that allows you to make consistently sized, even stitches. Aida cloth is the most popular of all cross-stitch fabrics. The threads are woven in groups separated by tiny spaces. This creates a pattern of squares across the surface of the fabric and enables even a beginning stitcher to easily identify exactly where to place the cross-stitches. Measure Aida cloth by squares per inch; for example, 14-count Aida cloth has 14 squares per inch.

Aida cloth comes in many varieties. Look for 100% Aida cloth in the following thread counts: 6, 8, 11, 14, 16, and 18. You'll find 14-count Aida cloth in more than 60 colors. For beginners, white Aida cloth is available with a removable grid of pre-basted threads.

Experienced stitchers consider linen to be the standard of excellence in fabric. The threads used to weave linen vary in thickness, giving linen fabrics a slightly irregular surface. When you purchase linen, remember to measure thread count by threads per inch. Most designs are worked over two threads, so 28-count linen will yield 14 stitches per inch. Linens are woven in counts from 14 to 40 threads per inch.

Due to the popularity of the craft, the market for specialty fabrics for counted cross-stitch continues to grown. These fabrics are referred to as even-weave because they're woven from threads with a consistent diameter, even though some fabrics have a homespun look. Count most even-weave fabrics as for linen, by threads per inch, and stitch over two threads of fabric.

Use Hardanger fabric for very fine counted cross-stitch. The traditional fabric for the Norwegian embroidery of the same name has an over-two, under-two weave that produces 22 small squares per inch.

Cross-stitch with needlepoint canvas on clothing and on other fabrics that aren't suitable for stitching alone. Specially designed waste canvas will unravel when dampened; it ranges in count from 6½ to 20 stitches per inch. You also can work cross-stitches directly on mono needlepoint canvas, available in several colors. Leave the background of your design unstitched for an interesting effect.

Work sweaters and other knits in duplicate stitches from cross-stitch charts. Knit stitches aren't square; they're wider than they are tall. A duplicate-stitched design will appear broader and shorter than the chart from which it was worked.

Gingham and other simple plaid fabrics also can be used for a cross-stitch background, but you'll find that gingham "squares" aren't perfectly square, so a stitched design will seem slightly taller and narrower than the chart.

Burlap fabric can easily be counted and stitched on as you would with any traditional counted-thread fabric.

Threads for Stitching

You can use most types of thread for counted cross-stitch embroidery projects. Six-ply cotton embroidery floss comes in the widest range of colors, including variegated colors. It separates easily into single or multiple plies for stitching.

Waste Canvas

Aida Cloth

Linen and Evenweave Fabrics

Pearl Cotton

Embroidery Floss

Silk Ribbons and Metallic Embroidery Ribbons

Beads

The instructions for each project in this book tell you how many plies to use. If you use a different fabric, use the chart on *page 124* as a guide, and experiment on a scrap of the fabric until you achieve the desired effect. A larger number of plies will result in a rich or heavy embroidered piece; a smaller number will create a light-weight or fragile texture.

Rayon and silk flosses are very similar in weight to six-ply cotton embroidery floss but have a greater sheen. Either can be interchanged with cotton floss, one ply for one ply, but because rayon and silk have a "slicker" texture, they're slightly more difficult to use.

You'll find pearl cotton in four sizes: #3, #5, #8, and #12 (#3 is thick; #12 is thin). Pearl cotton has an obvious twist and a high sheen.

Flower thread is a 100% cotton, matte-finish thread. Substitute a single strand of flower thread for two plies of cotton floss. Another product recently introduced on the market is overdyed threads. Most of the threads have an irregular, variegated, "one-of-a-kind" appearance. Cotton floss,

silk floss, flower thread, and pearl-cotton threads are available in this form. They produce a soft, shaded appearance without changing thread colors.

Specialty threads add a distinctive look to cross-stitch work. They range in weight from hair-fine blending filament, usually used with floss, to ⅛-inch-wide ribbon. Specialty threads include metallic threads, richly colored and textured threads, and fun to stitch, glow-in-the-dark threads.

Use wool yarn for cross-stitch as well as needlepoint or crewel embroidery. Use

one or two plies of three-ply Persian yarn, and select even-weave fabrics with fewer threads per inch when working cross-stitches in wool yarn.

Ribbon—silk, rayon, and polyester—provides an interesting texture for cross-stitching, especially in combination with flower-shaped embroidery stitches. Look for straight grain and bias-cut ribbons in solid and variegated colors and in widths ranging from 1/16 to 1½ inches.

Continued

Silk Floss

Metallic Threads

MATERIALS

Continued from page 123

Needle Types

Blunt-pointed needles are best for working on most cross-stitch fabrics because they slide through the holes and between threads without splitting or snagging the fibers. A large-eye needle accommodates most embroidery threads. Many companies sell special "cross-stitch" needles but they're identical to tapestry needles; both are blunt tipped and large-eyed. The convenient chart *below* will guide you to the right size needle for the most commonly used fabrics. One exception to the blunt-tip needle rule is waste canvas; use a sharp embroidery needle to work on that fabric.

Working with seed beads requires a very fine needle that will slide through the holes. Either a #8 quilting needle, which is short with a tiny eye, or a long beading needle, with a longer eye, will work. Some needlework shops also carry short beading needles with long eyes.

Fabrics, Needles, and Floss		
Fabric	Tapestry Needle Size	Number Of Plies
11-count	24	Three
14-count	24-26	Two
18-count	26	Two
22-count	26	One

GETTING STARTED

Cut the floss into 15- to 18-inch lengths and separate all six plies. Recombine the plies as indicated in the project instructions, and thread them into a blunt-tip needle. Refer to the project instructions for where to begin stitching the piece.

Basic Cross-Stitch

Make one cross-stitch for each symbol on the chart. For horizontal rows, stitch the first diagonal part of each stitch in the entire row. Then, work back across the row, completing the second diagonal part of each stitch. On most linen and even-weave fabrics, *work your stitches over two threads,* as shown in the diagram *below.* For Aida cloth, each stitch fills one square.

You also can work cross-stitches in the reverse direction. Just remember to embroider the stitches uniformly—that is, always work the top half of the stitch in the same direction.

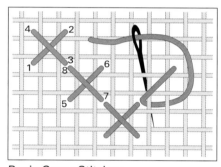

Basic Cross-Stitches
Worked Individually

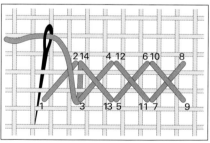

Basic Cross-Stitches in Rows

How to Secure Thread at the Beginning

The most common way to secure the beginning tail of the thread is to hold it under the first four or five stitches. Or, you can use a waste knot. Thread the needle, and knot the end of the thread.

Insert the needle from the right side of the fabric, about 4 inches away from the first stitch. Bring the needle up through the fabric, and work the first series of stitches. When you're finished, clip the knot on the right side. Pull the excess floss or thread to the wrong side of the fabric, and secure as in How to secure thread at end, *below.*

When you work with two, four, or six plies of floss, use a loop knot. Cut half as many plies of thread but make each one twice as long. Recombine the plies, fold the strand in half, and thread all of the ends into the needle. Work the first diagonal part of the first stitch, then, on the back, slip the needle through the loop formed by folding the thread.

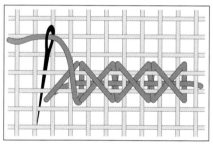

How to Secure Thread at the Beginning

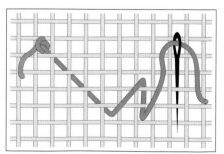

Waste Knot

How to Secure Thread at the End

To finish, slip the threaded needle under previously stitched threads on the wrong side of the fabric for four or five stitches, weaving the thread back and forth a few times. Clip the thread.

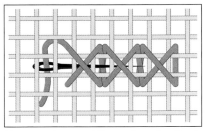

How to Secure Thread at the End

Half cross-stitch

A half cross-stitch is simply one single diagonal part, or half of a cross-stitch. Half cross-stitches usually are listed under a separate heading in the color key and are indicated on the chart by a colored diagonal line. The direction of the line indicates the desired direction of the stitch.

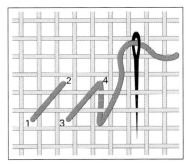

Half Cross-Stitch

Quarter and three-quarter cross-stitches

To obtain rounded shapes in a design, use quarter and three-quarter cross-stitches. On linen and even-weave fabrics, a quarter cross-stitch extends from the corner to the center intersection of the threads. To make quarter cross-stitches on Aida cloth, you'll have to estimate the center of the square. Three-quarter cross-stitches combine a quarter cross-stitch with a half cross-stitch.

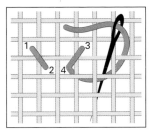

Quarter Cross-Stitch

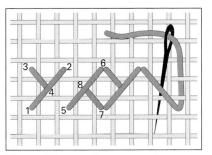

Three-Quarter Cross-Stitch

Cross-Stitch with Beads

When attaching beads with cross-stitches, work all first diagonal parts of the cross-stitches, then attach the beads when you work back across the row.

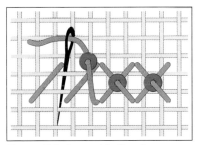

Cross-Stitches with Beads

Backstitches

Backstitches are added to define and outline the shapes in a design. For most cross-stitch projects, backstitches require only one ply of floss. On the color key, (2X) behind the mention of a certain area indicates you should backstitch with two plies of floss, (3X) indicates three plies, etc.

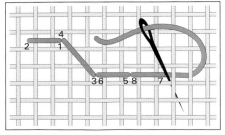

Backstitch

French Knot

Bring the threaded needle up through the fabric, and wrap the floss around the needle as illustrated. Tighten the twists, and insert the needle back through the fabric in the same place. The floss will slide through the wrapped thread to make the knot. Do not pull the thread too tight or you'll pull the knot out.

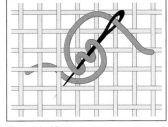

French Knot

Whipstitch

A whipstitch is an overcast stitch often used to finish the edges of perforated plastic. Pull each whipstitch tight for a neat finished appearance. You can also use whipstitches to join two fabrics together.

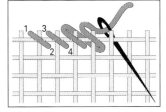

Whipstitch

INDEX

Country Christmas Afghan, page 11

Country Christmas Sampler, page 51

Santa Pins, page 83

SOURCES AND SUPPLIERS

Many of the materials and items used in this book are available at crafts and needlework stores. For more information, write or call the manufacturers below.

Chapter 1
Making Spirits Bright
Page 7, Merry Christmas Sampler: White linen—Wichelt Imports, Inc., Rte. 1, Stoddard, WI 54658.

Merry Christmas Sampler, page 7

Page 8, Sleigh Stocking: White Aida cloth—Charles Craft, P.O. Box 1049, Laurinburg, NC 28353; Cord—Heritage Trimming, Parade Hill Rd., Barnstead, NH 03218, 603/435-6795; Jingle bells—Darice, Inc., 21160 Drake Rd., Strongsville, OH 44136-6699.

Page 9, Merry Christmas Banner: Valerie fabric—Zweigart, 2 Riverview Dr., Somerset, NJ 08873-1139, 908/271-1949; Variegated floss—DMC, Port Kearney Bldg. 10, South Kearney, NJ 07032-0650; Metallic threads—Kreinik Manufacturing-Daisy Chain, P.O. Box 1258, Parkersburg, WV 26102, 304/428-9500; Quilt batting—Fairfield Processing Corp., P.O. Box 1157, Danbury, CT 06813; Jingle bells—Darice, Inc.

Page 11, Country Christmas Afghan: Lady Elizabeth afghan—Charles Craft, P.O. Box 1049, Laurinburg, NC 28343; Satin ribbon—C.M. Offray & Sons, Inc., Rte. 24 Box 601, Chester, NJ 07930; 908/879-4700; Metallic threads—Kreinik Manufacturing.

Chapter 2
Gifts of Good Taste
Pages 24, Popcorn, Peppermint Candy, and Ho-Ho Santa Banding: Banding—Zweigart.

Page 26, Christmas Rose Place Mat, Napkin, and Jar Topper: Royal Classic place mat and napkin—Charles Craft; Satin ribbon—C.M. Offray & Sons.

Santa, Snowman, and Teddy Gift Bags, page 27

Page 27, Santa, Snowman, and Teddy Gift Bags: Jobelan fabric—Wichelt Imports, Inc.

Chapter 3
A Story to Stitch
Pages 32–33, Nativity: Jobelan fabric—Wichelt Imports, Inc.; Metallic threads—Kreinik Manufacturing.

Chapter 4
Country Comforts
Page 51, Country Christmas Sampler: Fiddler's Lite Aida cloth—Charles Craft.

Page 52, Snowman Hostess Set: Royal Classic place mat and napkin—Charles Craft; Estate towel—Charles Craft; White-and-blue Aida banding—Zweigart.

Snowman Hostess Set, page 52

Page 53, Mini Band Sampler: Red-on-raw linen banding—Zweigart; Metallic threads—Kreinik Manufacturing; Charms—Creative Beginnings, 475 Morro Bay Blvd., Morro Bay, CA 93442.

Page 54, Cat and Mouse Stocking: Christmas-green pearl Aida cloth—Zweigart; Piping—Hollywood Trims, 42005 Cook St., Suite 106, Palm Desert, CA 92260; Seed beads—Mill Hill Beads, 800/447-1332.

Page 55, Winter Wonderland Sampler and Pillow: Navy Heatherfield fabric—Wichelt Imports, Inc.; Polyester fiberfill—Fairfield Processing Corp.

Chapter 5
Deck the Boughs
Pages 64–65, Country Christmas ornaments and cards: White perforated paper—Yarn Tree Designs; Metallic thread—Kreinik Manufacturing; Seed beads—Mill Hill Beads; Acrylic paint—Delta Technical Coatings, 2550 Pellissier Pl., Whittier, CA 90601-1505, 800/423-4135; Greeting cards—Yarn Tree Designs; Felt—Kunin Felt, 380 Lafayette Rd., Box 5000, Hampton, NH 03843-5000; Metallic gold cord—Heritage Trimming.

Page 66, Elf Ornaments: Ivory Aida cloth—Zweigart; Polyester fiberfill—Fairfield Processing Corp.

Page 68, Beaded Snowflake Ornaments: Silver perforated paper—Yarn Tree Designs; Seed beads—Mill Hill Beads; Braid—Kreinik Manufacturing.

Page 69, Pipecleaner Elves: White perforated paper—Yarn Tree Designs, 117 Alexander St., P.O. Box 724, Ames, IA 50010, 800/247-3952; Metallic threads—Kreinik Manufacturing; Jingle bells—Darice, Inc.

Page 70, Nutcracker Ornament: Monaco fabric—Charles Craft; Metallic threads—Kreinik Manufacturing; Seed beads—Mill Hill Beads; Cord—Heritage Trimming; Polyester fiberfill—Fairfield Processing Corp.

Continued

Continued from page 127

Page 71, Snowflake Medallion Ornaments: White Murano fabric—Wichelt Imports, Inc.; Felt—Kunin Felt; Metallic threads—Kreinik Manufacturing; Gold braid and Red-and-gold trim—Heritage Trimming.

Chapter 6
Santa Magic
Page 81, St. Nick: White Brittney fabric—Zweigart; Metallic thread—Kreinik Manufacturing.
Page 82, Hot-Air Balloon Santa: White Aida cloth—Zweigart.

Hot-Air Balloon Santa, page 82

Page 83, Down the Chimney Pin: Clear perforated plastic—Darice, Inc.; Braid—Kreinik Manufacturing; Seed beads—Mill Hill Beads; Felt—Kunin Felt.
Page 83, Santa Ringer Pin: Clear perforated plastic—Darice, Inc.; Waterlilies cotton thread—The Caron Collection, 67 Poland St., Bridgeport, CT 06605; Braid—Kreinik Manufacturing; Seed beads—Mill Hill Beads; Felt—Kunin Felt.
Page 84, Santa Garland: White perforated paper—Yarn Tree Designs.
Page 85, Santa Tree Topper: Moss-green Jobelan fabric—Wichelt Imports, Inc.; Metallic thread—Kreinik Manufacturing; Clear plastic canvas—Darice, Inc.

Chapter 7
Symbols of the Season
Page 95, Angel Table Runner and Napkin: Mushroom Lugana fabric—Zweigart; Metallic thread—Kreinik Manufacturing.

Page 97, Poinsettia Towel and Napkin: Towel and Royal Classic napkin—Charles Craft; Metallic thread—Kreinik Manufacturing.
Page 97, Christmas Bells Napkin and Pot Holder: Royal Classic napkin and pot holder—Charles Craft; Metallic thread—DMC.

Christmas Bells Napkin and Pot Holder, page 97

Page 98, "All Hearts Come Home for Christmas" Sampler: Cream-and-Gold Lugana fabric—Zweigart; Metallic gold thread—Rainbow Gallery Fibers, 7412 Fulton Ave. #5, North Hollywood, VA 91605; Pearl cotton—DMC.

Chapter 8
Dressed in Holiday Style
Page 107, Christmas Rose Blouse: Metallic thread—Kreinik Manufacturing; Silk ribbon—YLI Corporation, 800/854-1932.
Page 108, Elegant Bag: Mushroom Lugana fabric—Zweigart; Metallic threads—Kreinik Manufacturing; Pearl cotton—DMC; Cord—Heritage Trimming; Wooden bead—Westrim Crafts, available at crafts stores.
Page 110, Christmas Kitten Collar: Cherub-pink Royal Danish linen—Wichelt Imports, Inc.; Metallic thread—Kreinik Manufacturing; Petite seed beads—Mill Hill Beads; Satin ribbon—C.M. Offray & Sons.
Page 111, Tree-Trimmin' Teddy Vest: Country Oatmeal Royal Classic fabric—Charles Craft.

Fabrics
Charles Craft, P.O. Box 1049, Laurinberg, NC 28353, 800/277-0980;
Wichelt Imports, Inc., R.R. 1, Stoddard, WI 54658;
Zweigart, 2 Riverview Dr., Somerset, NJ 08873-1139, 908/271-1949.

Threads
Anchor, Consumer Service Dept., P.O. Box 27067, Greenville, SC 29616;
DMC, Port Kearney Bldg. 10, South Kearney, NJ 07032-0650;
Kreinik Manufacturing, Daisy Chain, P.O. Box 1258, Parkersburg, WV 26102, 800/537-2166;
The Caron Collection, 67 Poland St., Bridgeport, CT 06605;
Rainbow Gallery Fibers, 7412 Fulton Ave. #5, North Hollywood, CA 91605;
YLI Corporation, 800/854-1932.

Trims
Creative Beginnings, 475 Morro Bay Blvd., Morro Bay, CA 93442;
Darice, Inc., 21160 Drake Rd., Strongsville, OH 44136-6699;
Heritage Trimming, Parade Hill Rd., Barnstead, NH 03218, 603/435-6795;
C.M. Offray & Sons, Inc., Rte. 24 Box 601, Chester, NJ 07930; 908/879-4700;
Yarn Tree Designs, 117 Alexander St., P.O. Box 724, Ames, IA 50010, 800/247-3952;
Hollywood Trims, 42005 Cook St., Suite 106, Palm Desert, CA 92260;
Mill Hill Beads, 800/447-1332.
Delta Technical Coatings, 2550 Pellissier Pl., Whittier, CA 90601-1505, 800/423-4135.

Framing
Dot's Frame Shop, 4223 Fleur Dr., Des Moines, IA 50321.

Photographs
Marcia Cameron
Pages 36-37, 39, 40, 42, and 44-45.
Scott Little
Cover, and pages 7, 8, 9, 11, 24-25, 26, 27, 32, 51-55, 64-65, 66, 67, 68, 69, 70, 71, 81, 82, 83, 84, 85, 95, 97, 98, 107, 108, 110, and 111.
Perry Struse
Pages 3, 69, and 75.